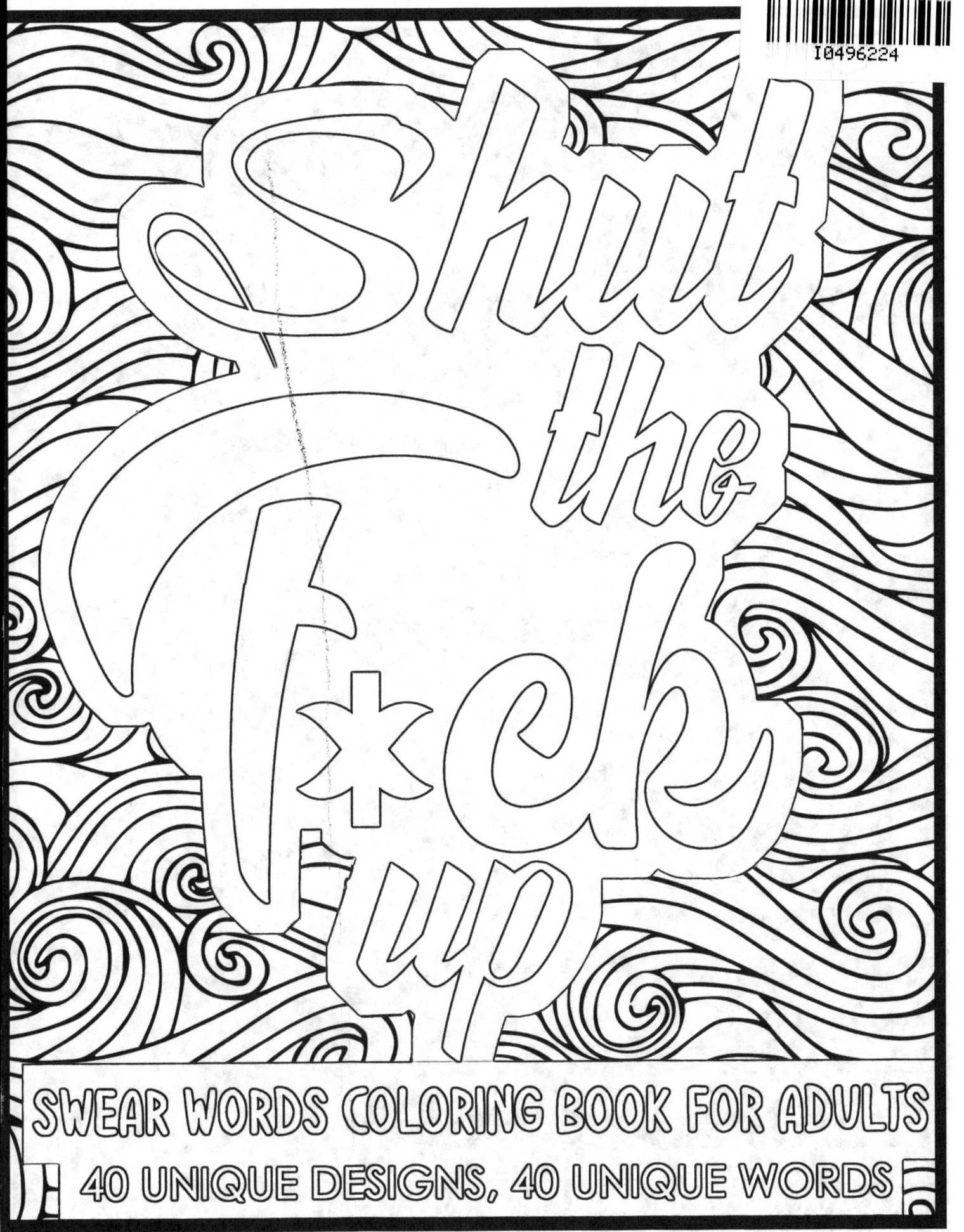

**THE PAGES ON THE LEFT ARE BLACK-BACKED
TO AVOID COLOR BLEEDING TO THE NEXT PAGE.**

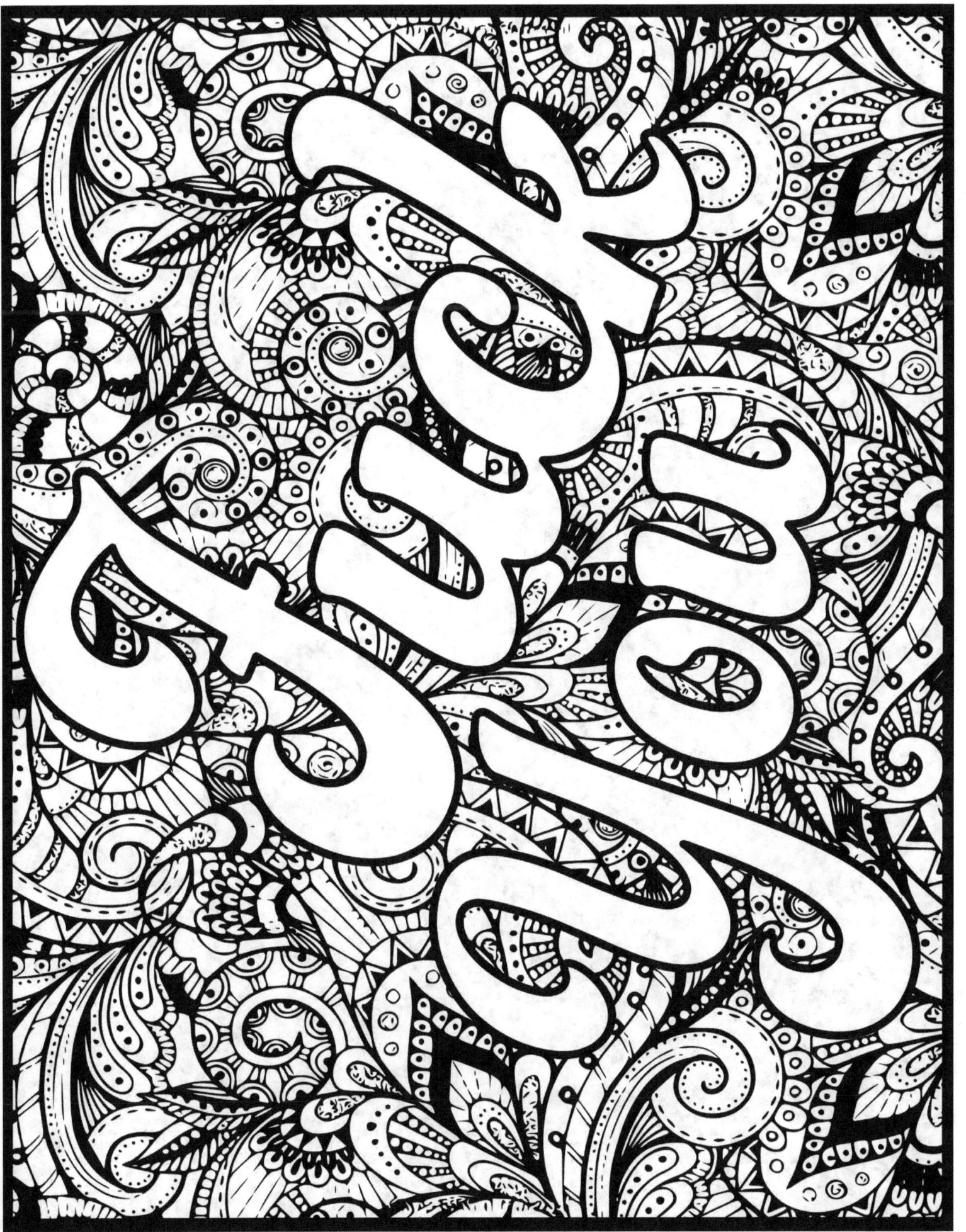

THE PAGES ON THE LEFT ARE BLACK-BACKED
TO AVOID COLOR BLEEDING TO THE NEXT PAGE.

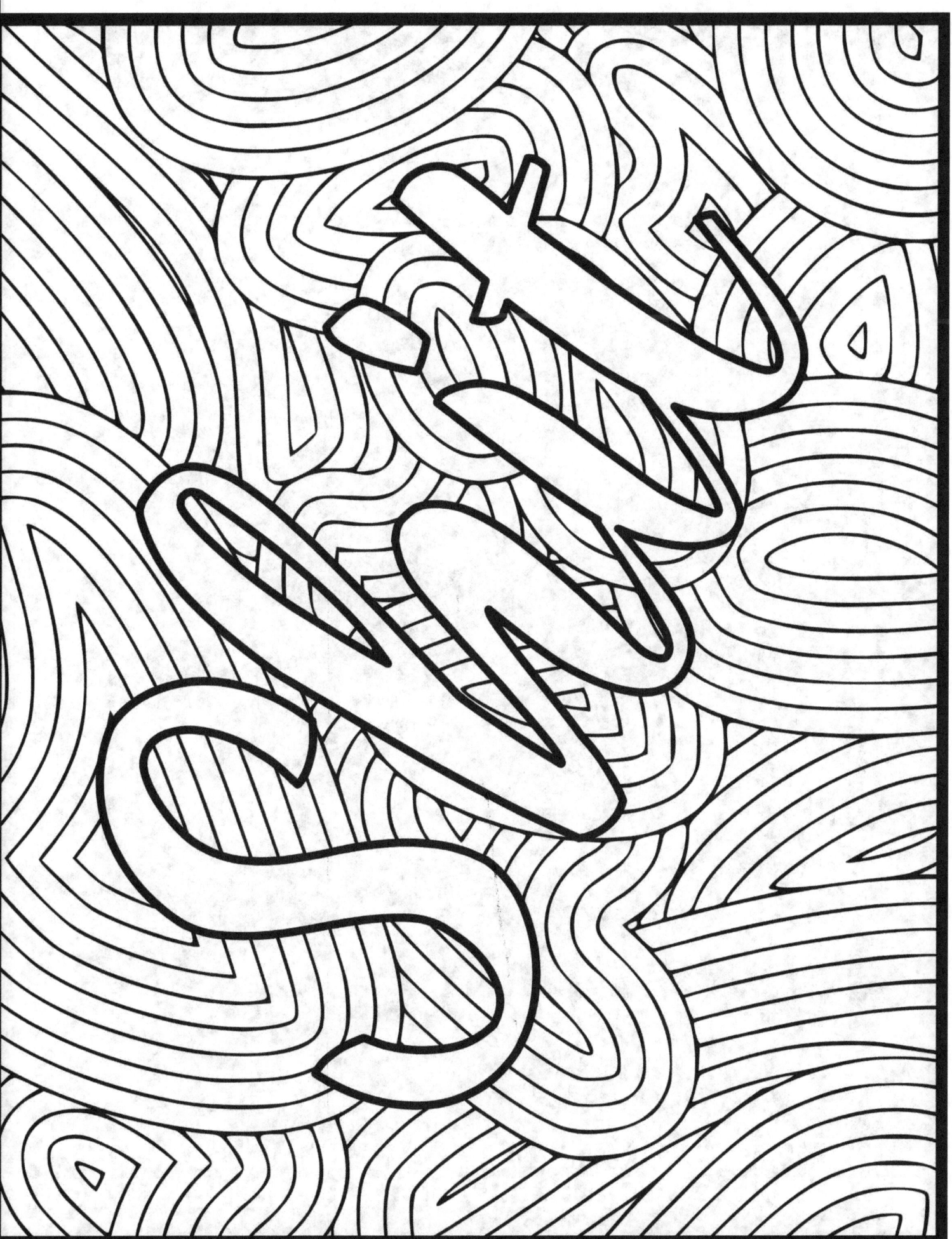

THE PAGES ON THE LEFT ARE BLACK-BACKED TO AVOID COLOR BLEEDING TO THE NEXT PAGE.

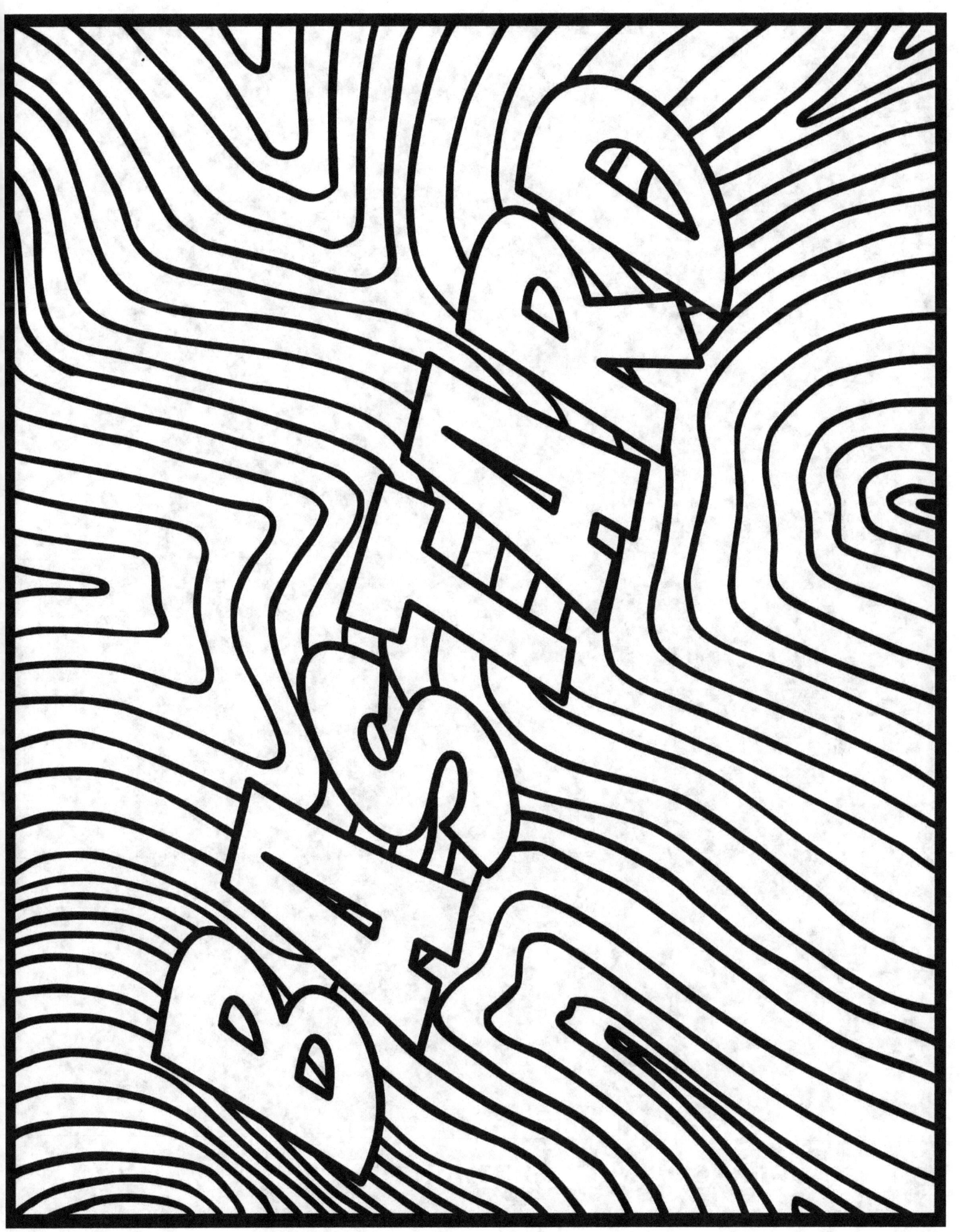

THE PAGES ON THE LEFT ARE BLACK-BACKED TO AVOID COLOR BLEEDING TO THE NEXT PAGE.

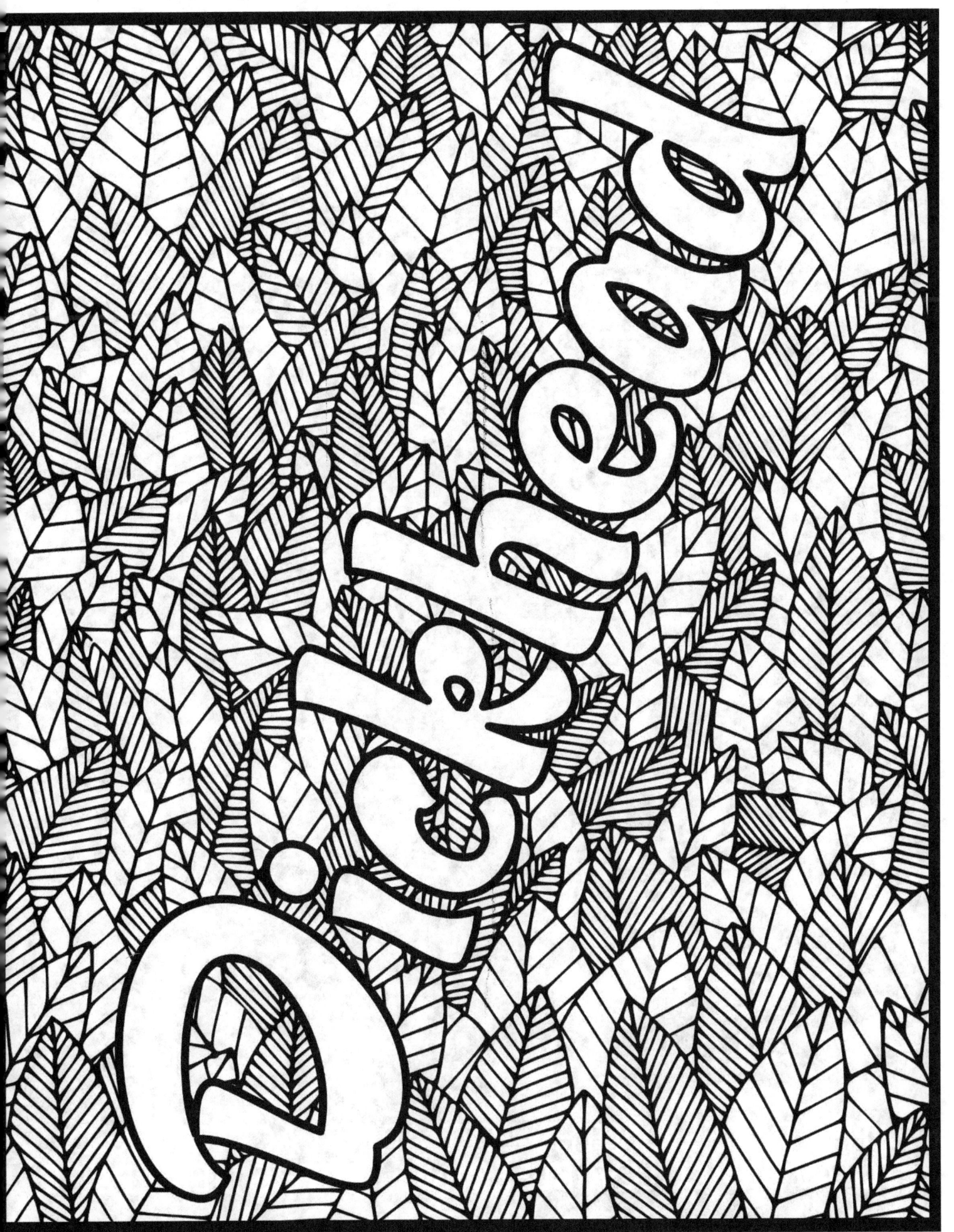

THE PAGES ON THE LEFT ARE BLACK-BACKED
TO AVOID COLOR BLEEDING TO THE NEXT PAGE.

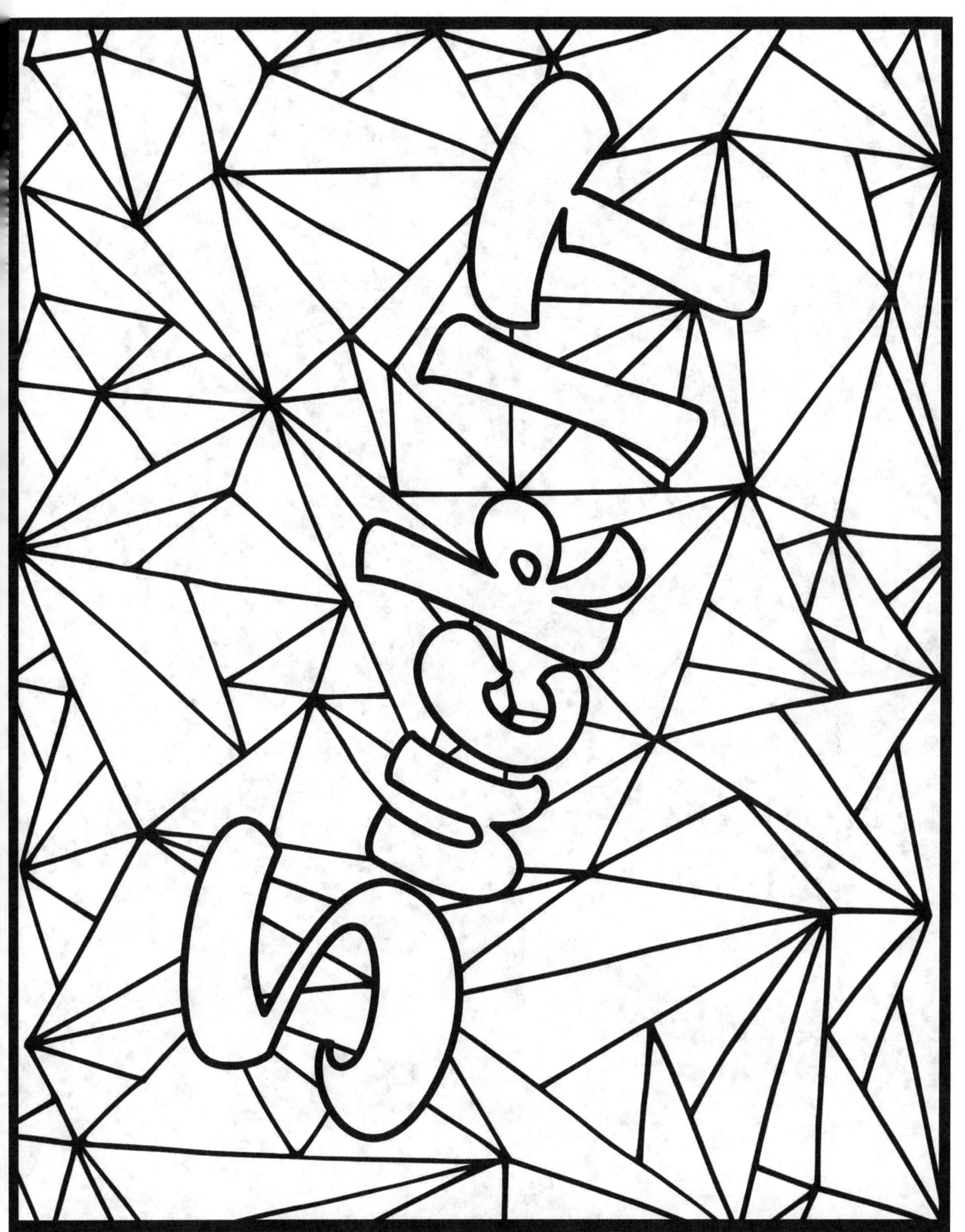

THE PAGES ON THE LEFT ARE BLACK-BACKED
TO AVOID COLOR BLEEDING TO THE NEXT PAGE.

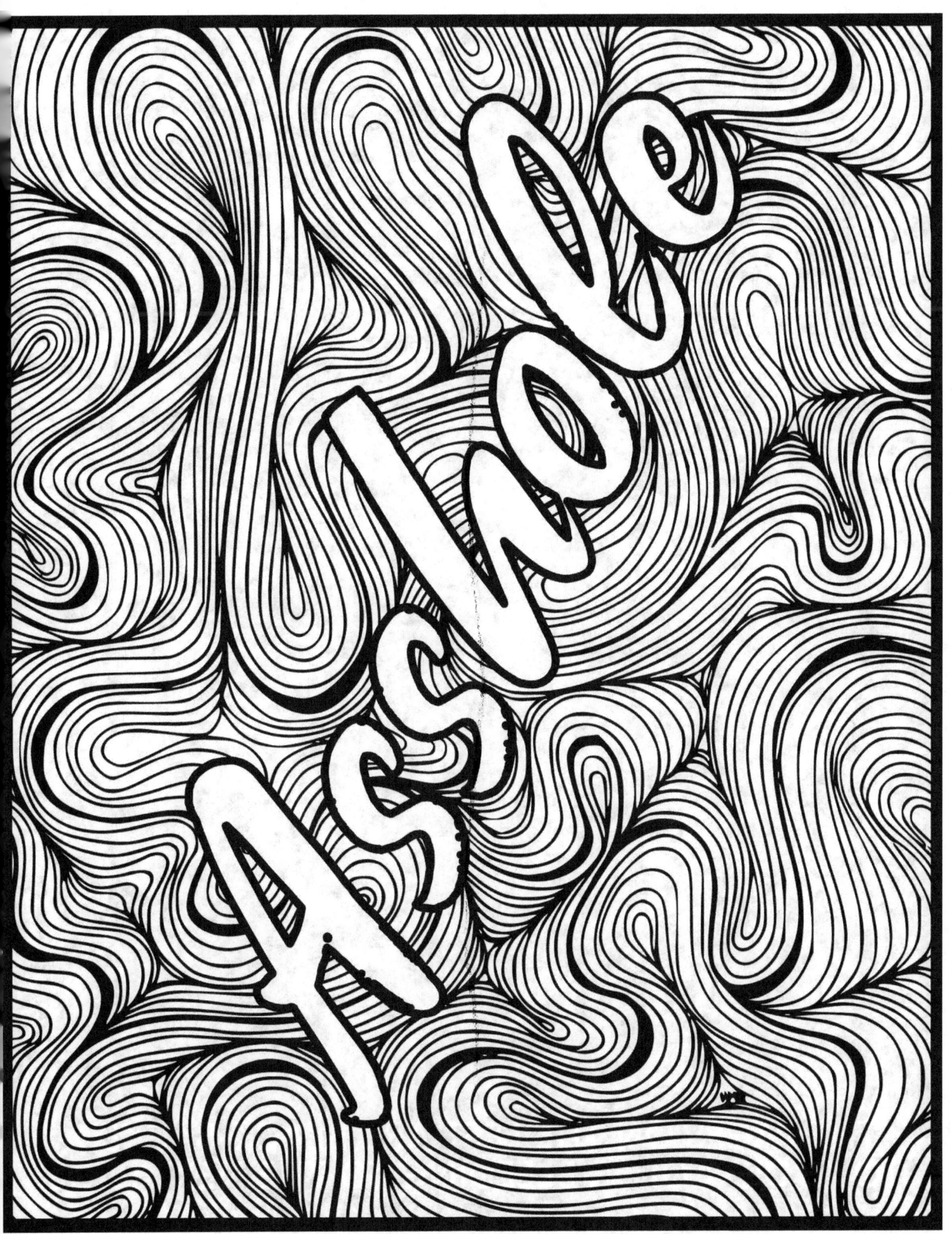

THE PAGES ON THE LEFT ARE BLACK-BACKED TO AVOID COLOR BLEEDING TO THE NEXT PAGE.

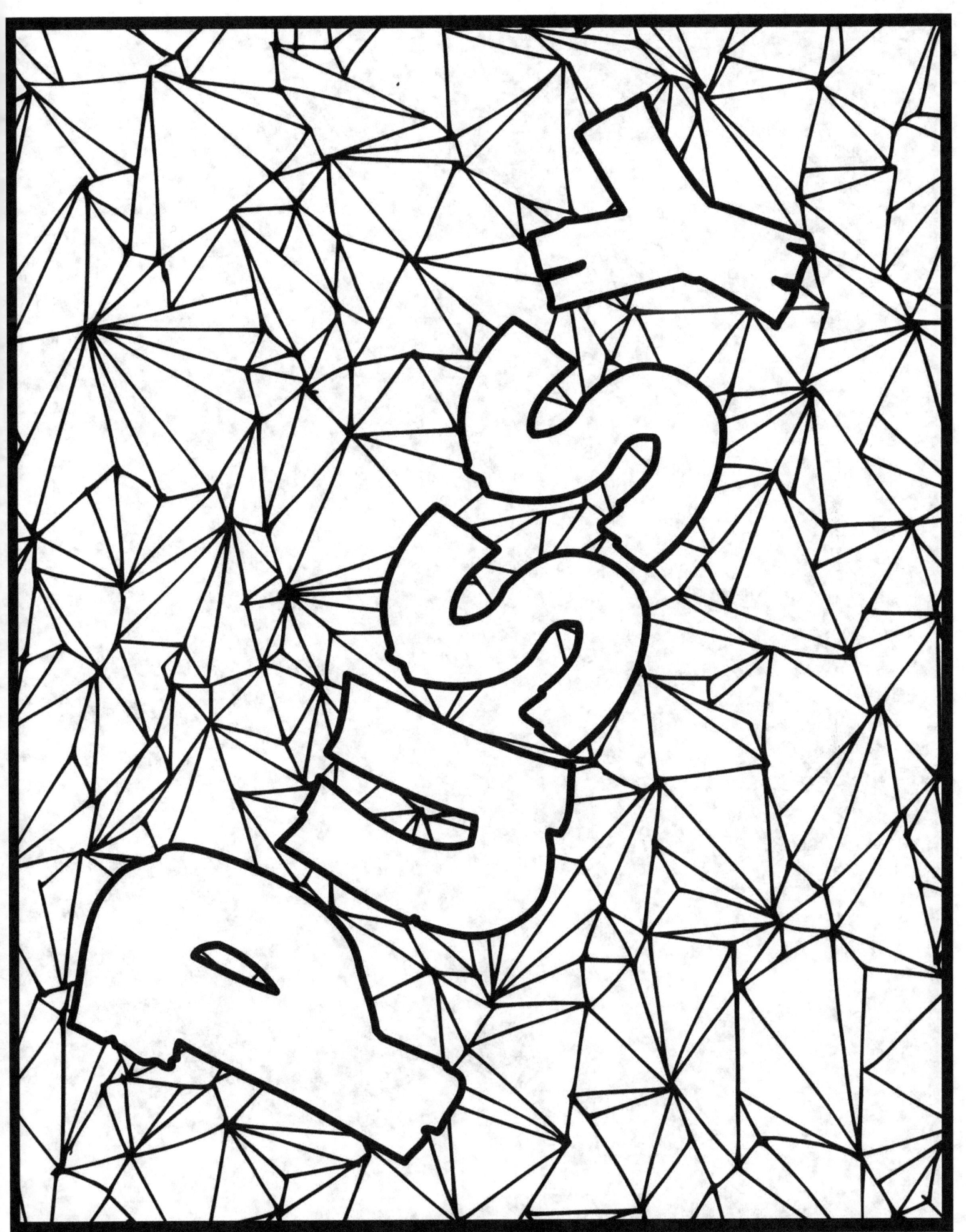

THE PAGES ON THE LEFT ARE BLACK-BACKED
TO AVOID COLOR BLEEDING TO THE NEXT PAGE.

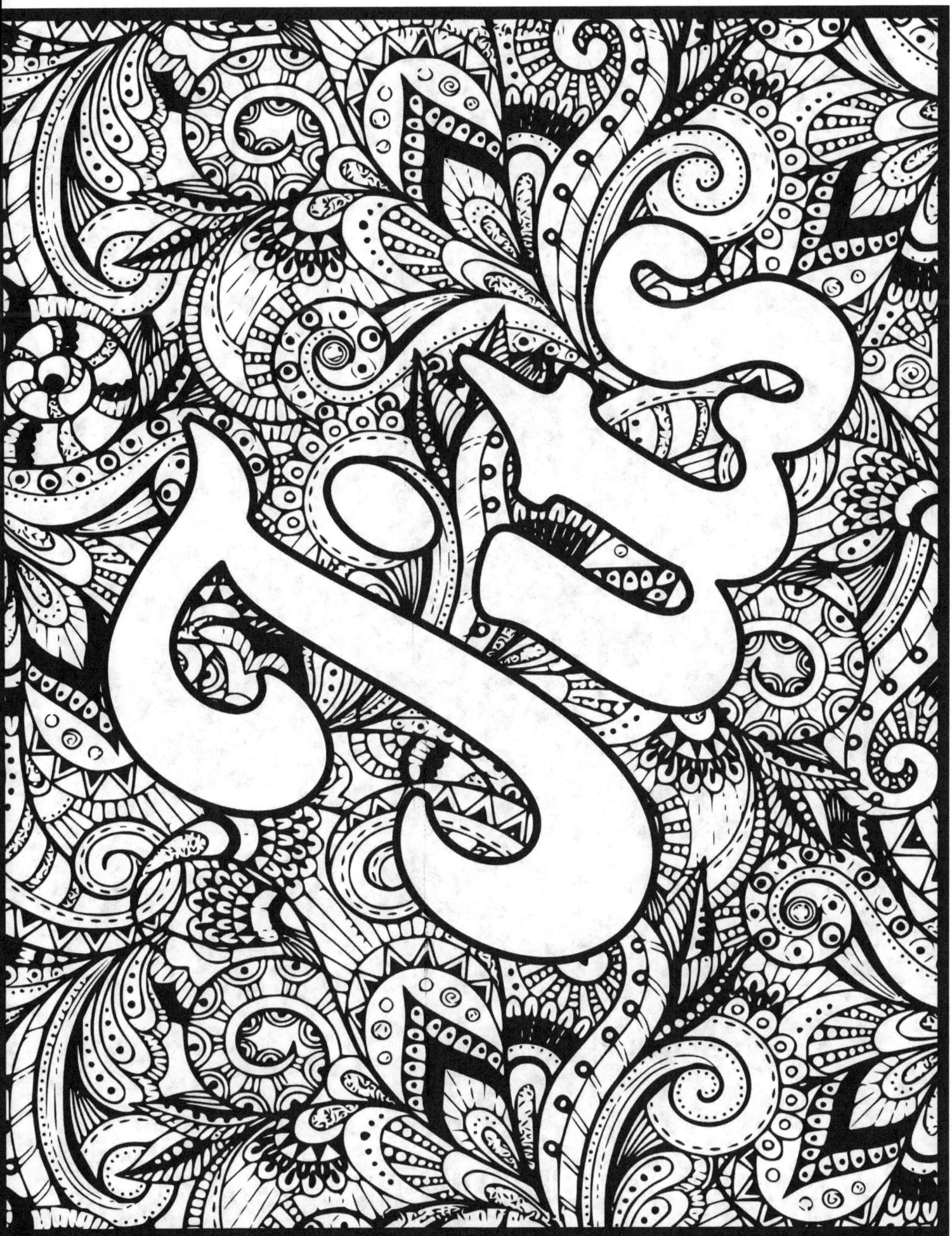

THE PAGES ON THE LEFT ARE BLACK-BACKED
TO AVOID COLOR BLEEDING TO THE NEXT PAGE.

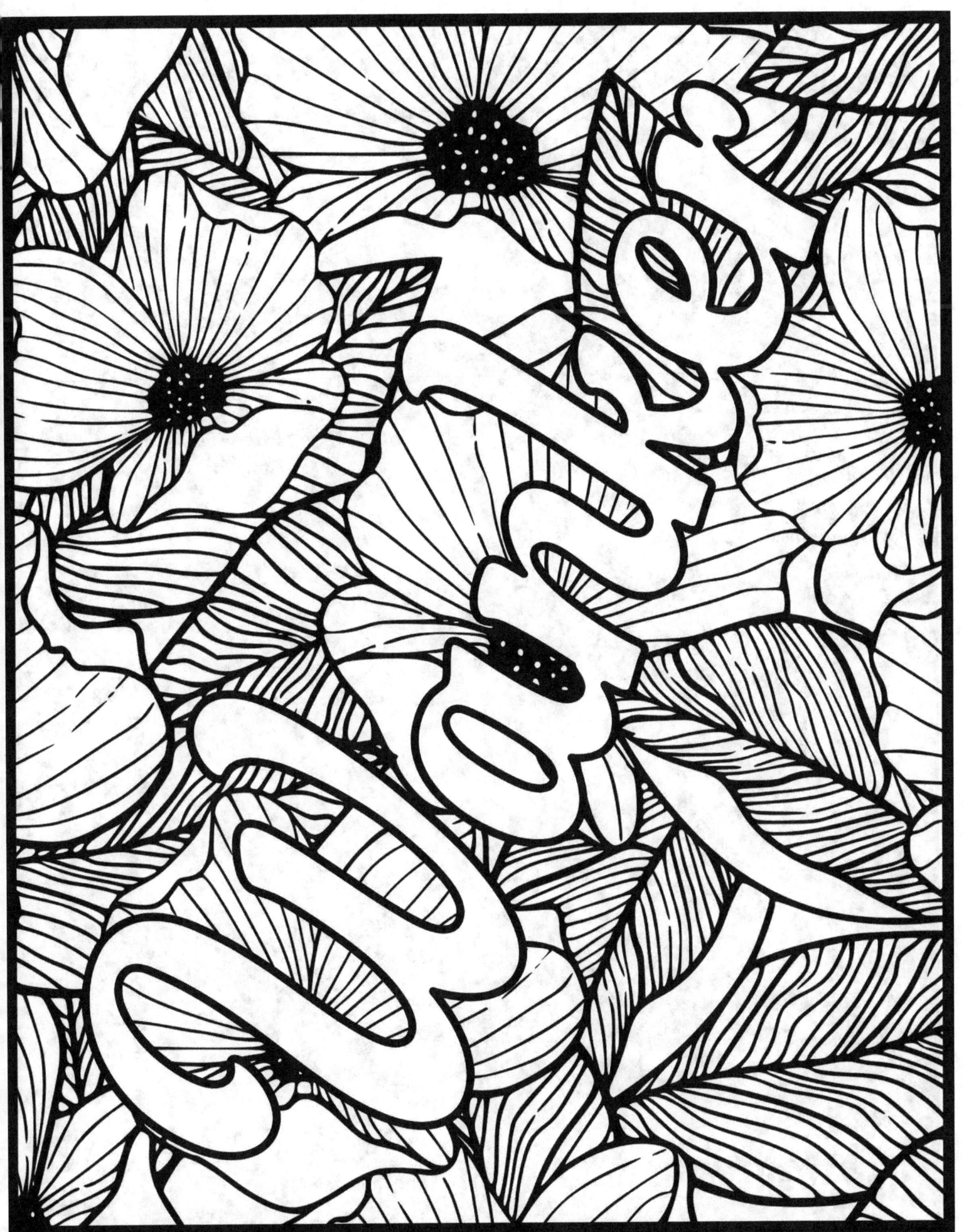

THE PAGES ON THE LEFT ARE BLACK-BACKED
TO AVOID COLOR BLEEDING TO THE NEXT PAGE.

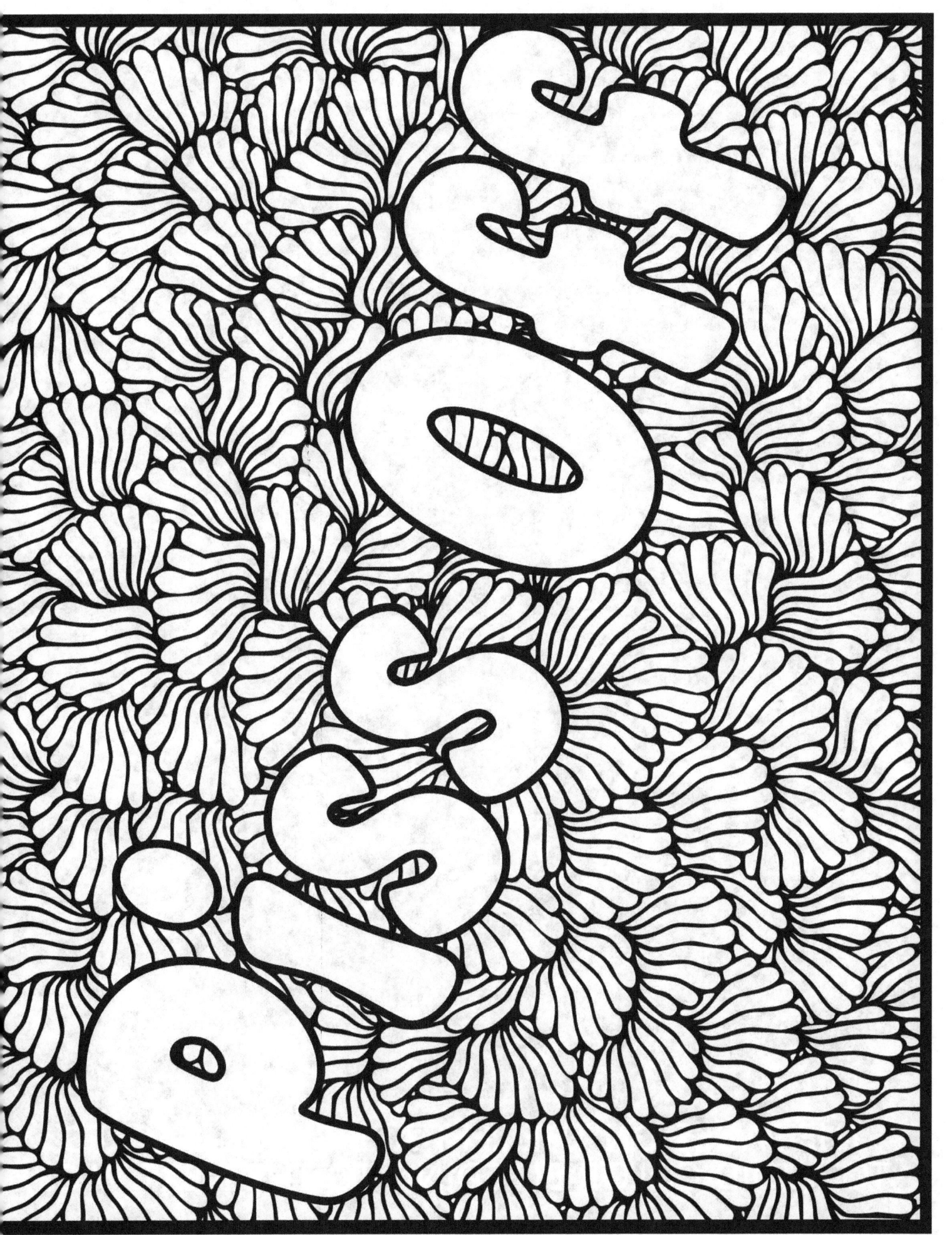

THE PAGES ON THE LEFT ARE BLACK-BACKED TO AVOID COLOR BLEEDING TO THE NEXT PAGE.

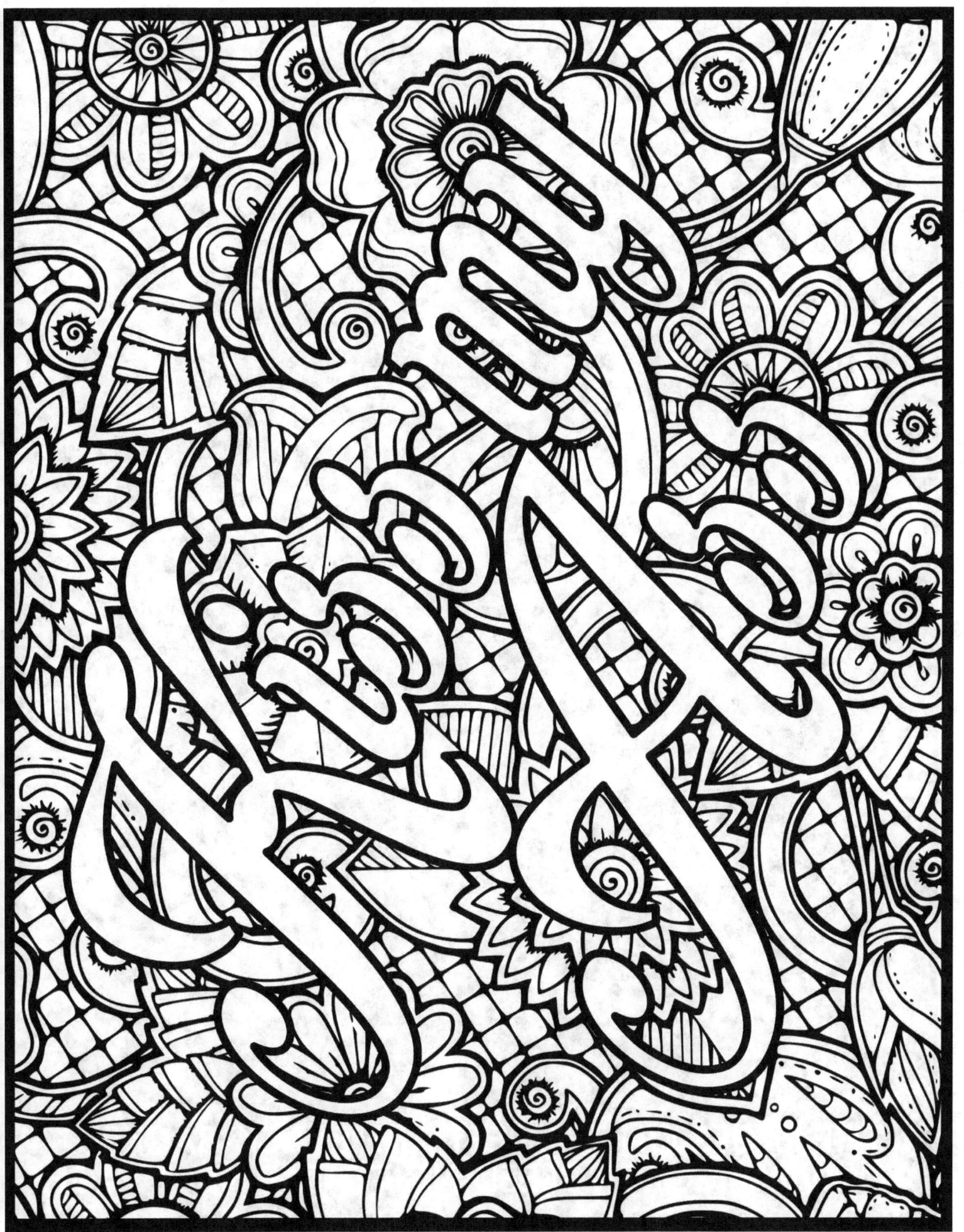

THE PAGES ON THE LEFT ARE BLACK-BACKED
TO AVOID COLOR BLEEDING TO THE NEXT PAGE.

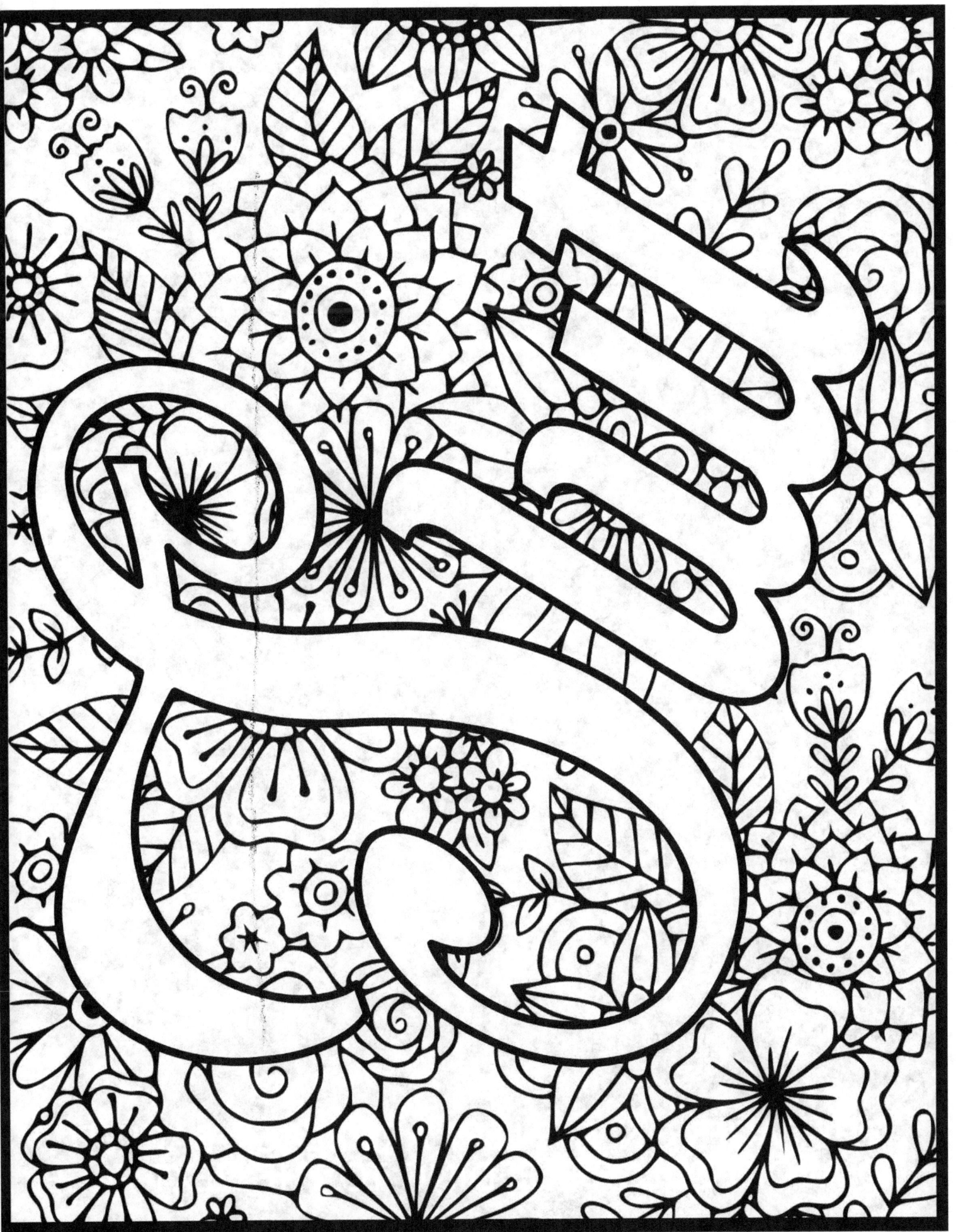

THE PAGES ON THE LEFT ARE BLACK-BACKED
TO AVOID COLOR BLEEDING TO THE NEXT PAGE.

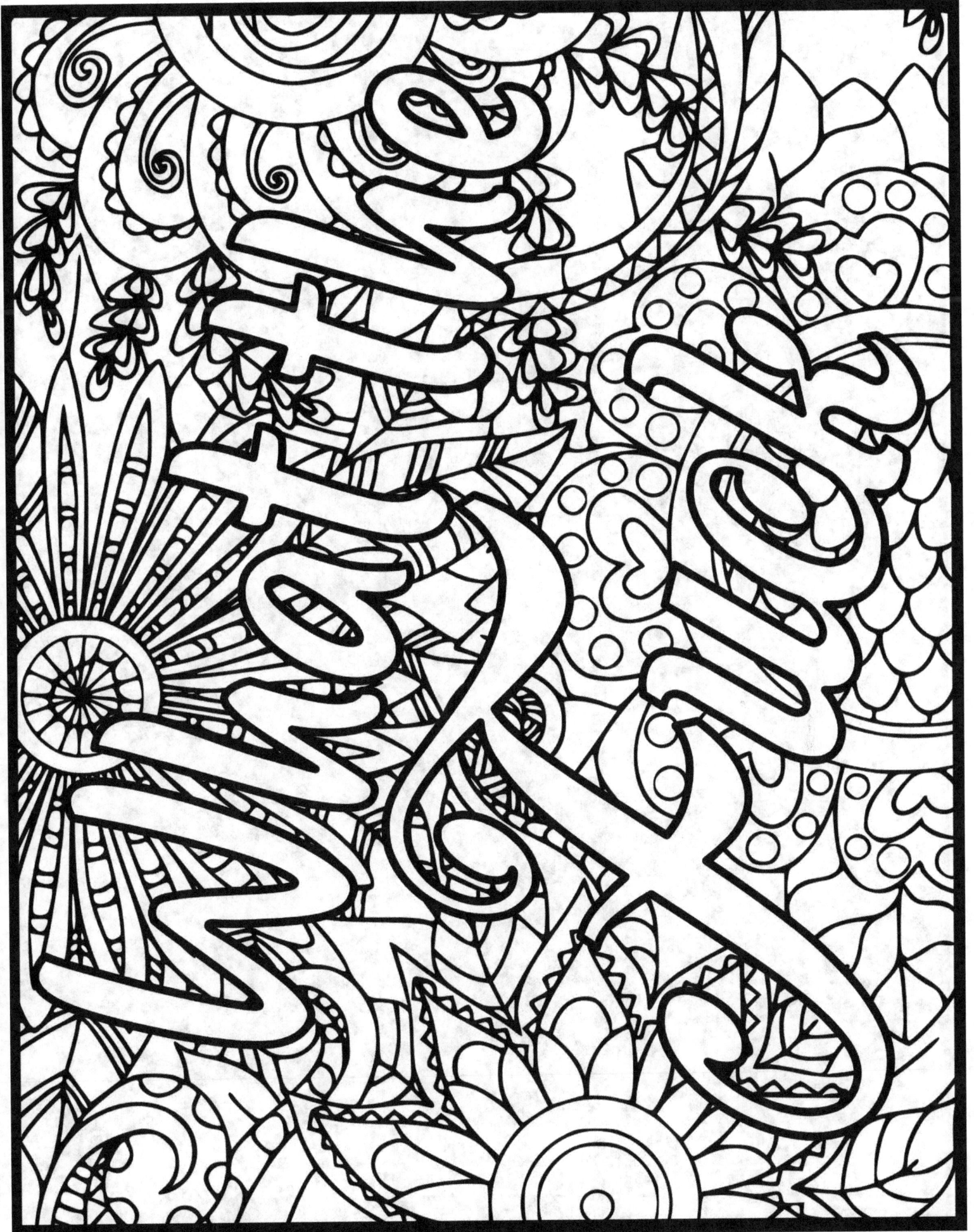

THE PAGES ON THE LEFT ARE BLACK-BACKED TO AVOID COLOR BLEEDING TO THE NEXT PAGE.

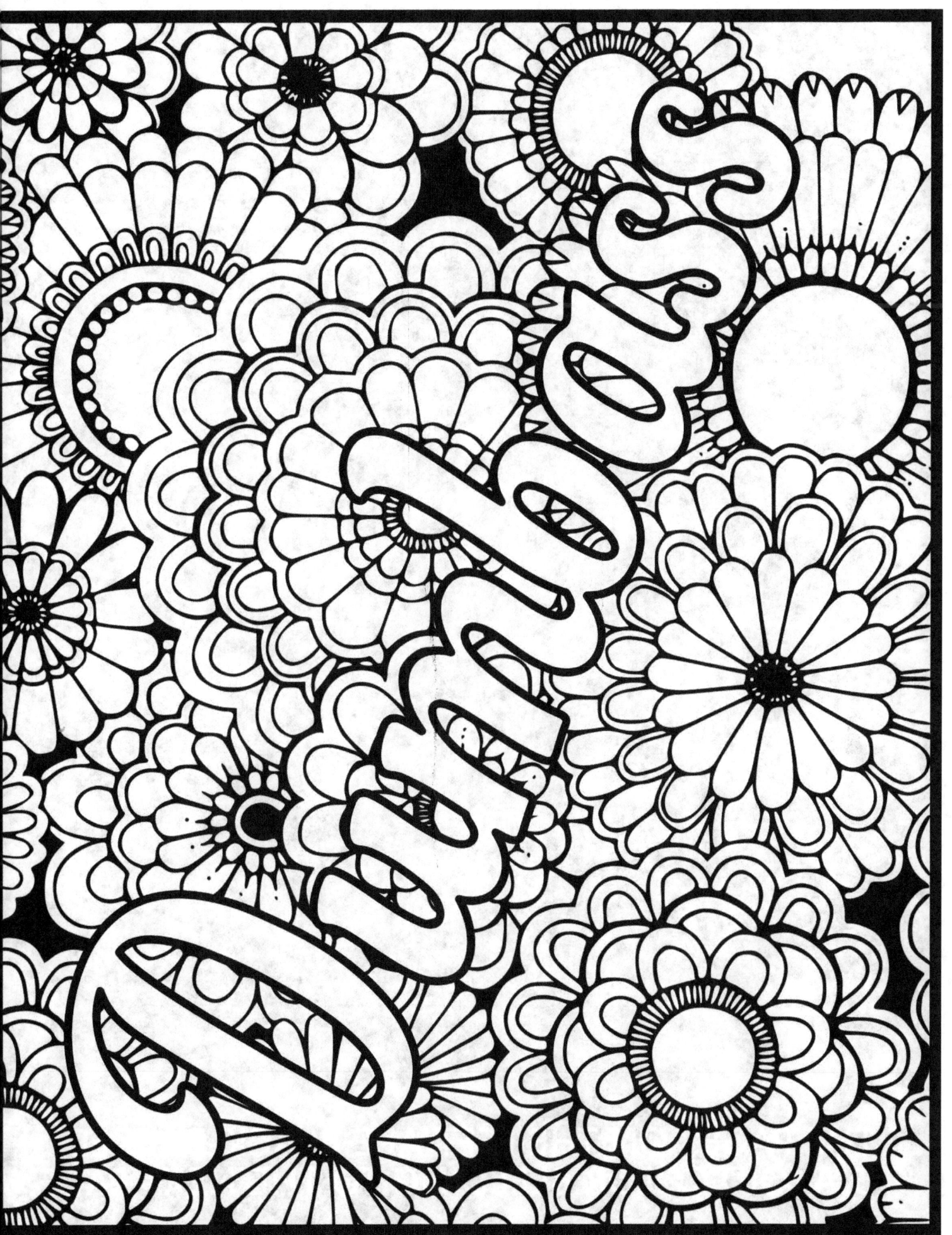

THE PAGES ON THE LEFT ARE BLACK-BACKED
TO AVOID COLOR BLEEDING TO THE NEXT PAGE.

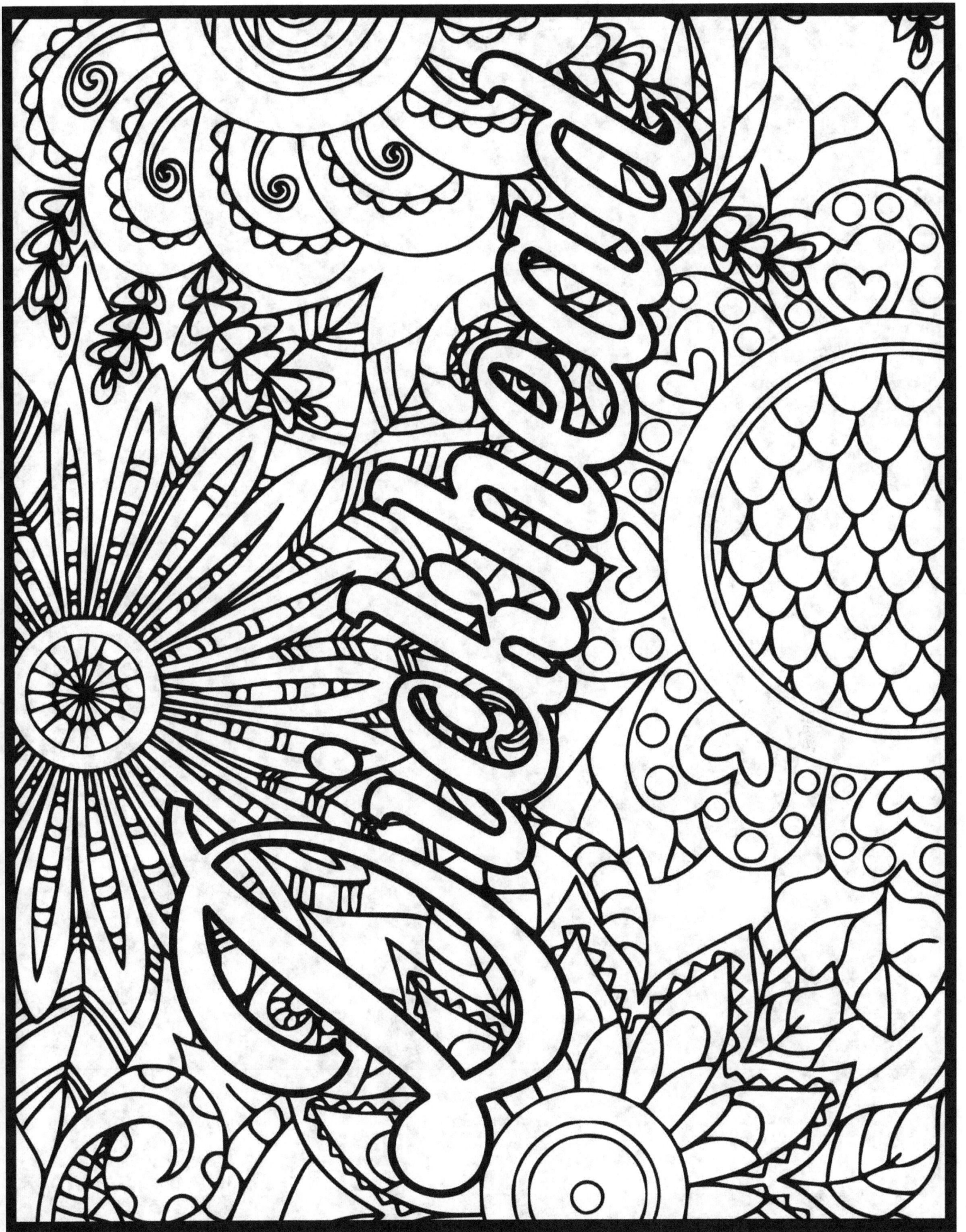

THE PAGES ON THE LEFT ARE BLACK-BACKED
TO AVOID COLOR BLEEDING TO THE NEXT PAGE.

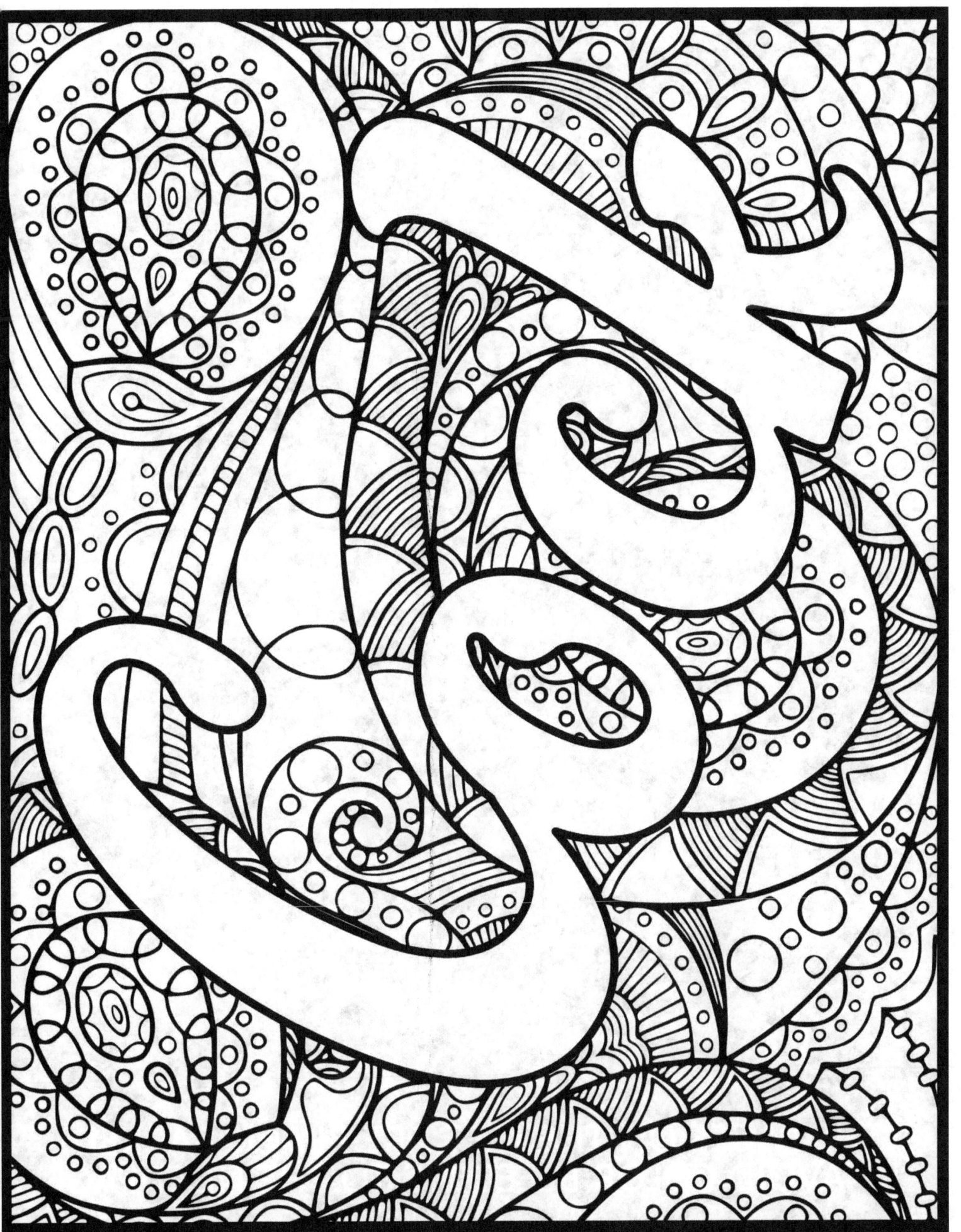

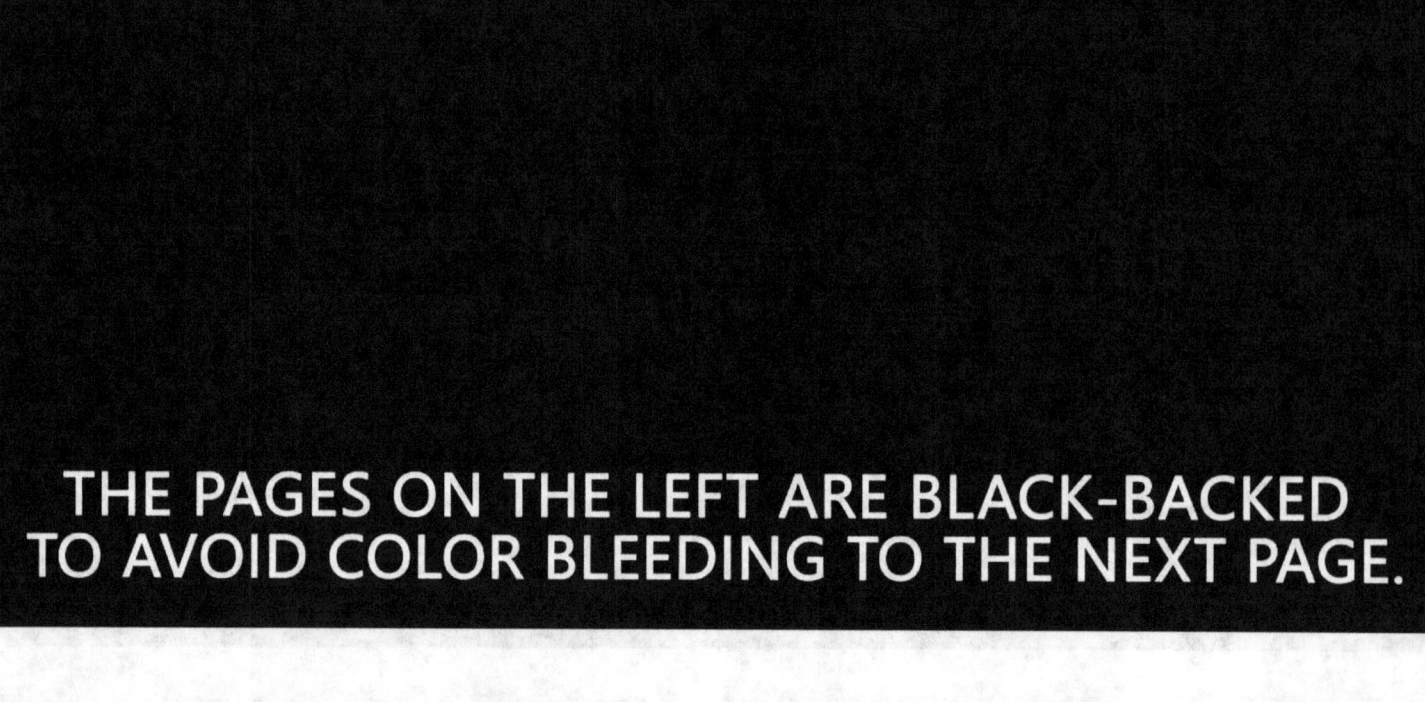

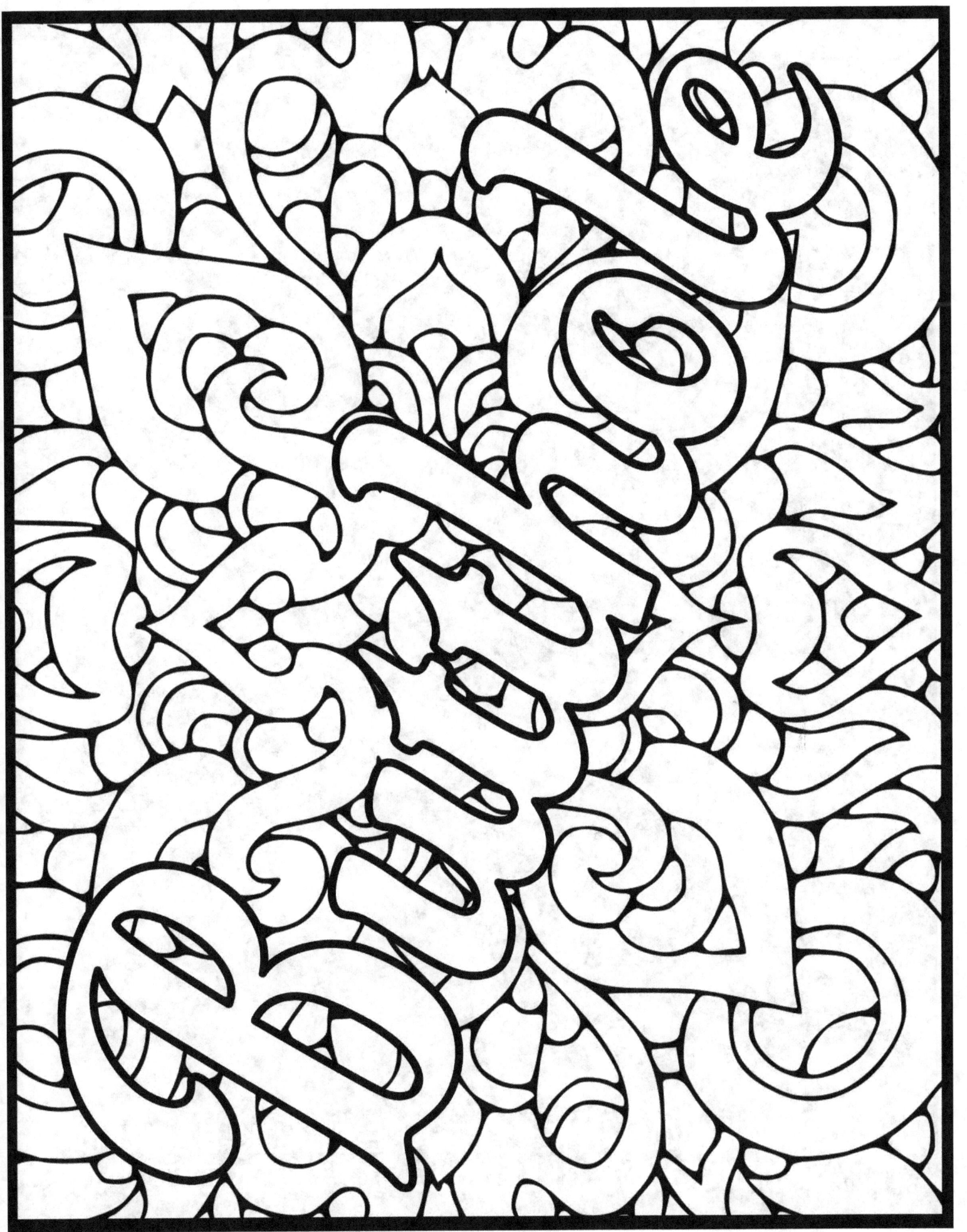

THE PAGES ON THE LEFT ARE BLACK-BACKED
TO AVOID COLOR BLEEDING TO THE NEXT PAGE.

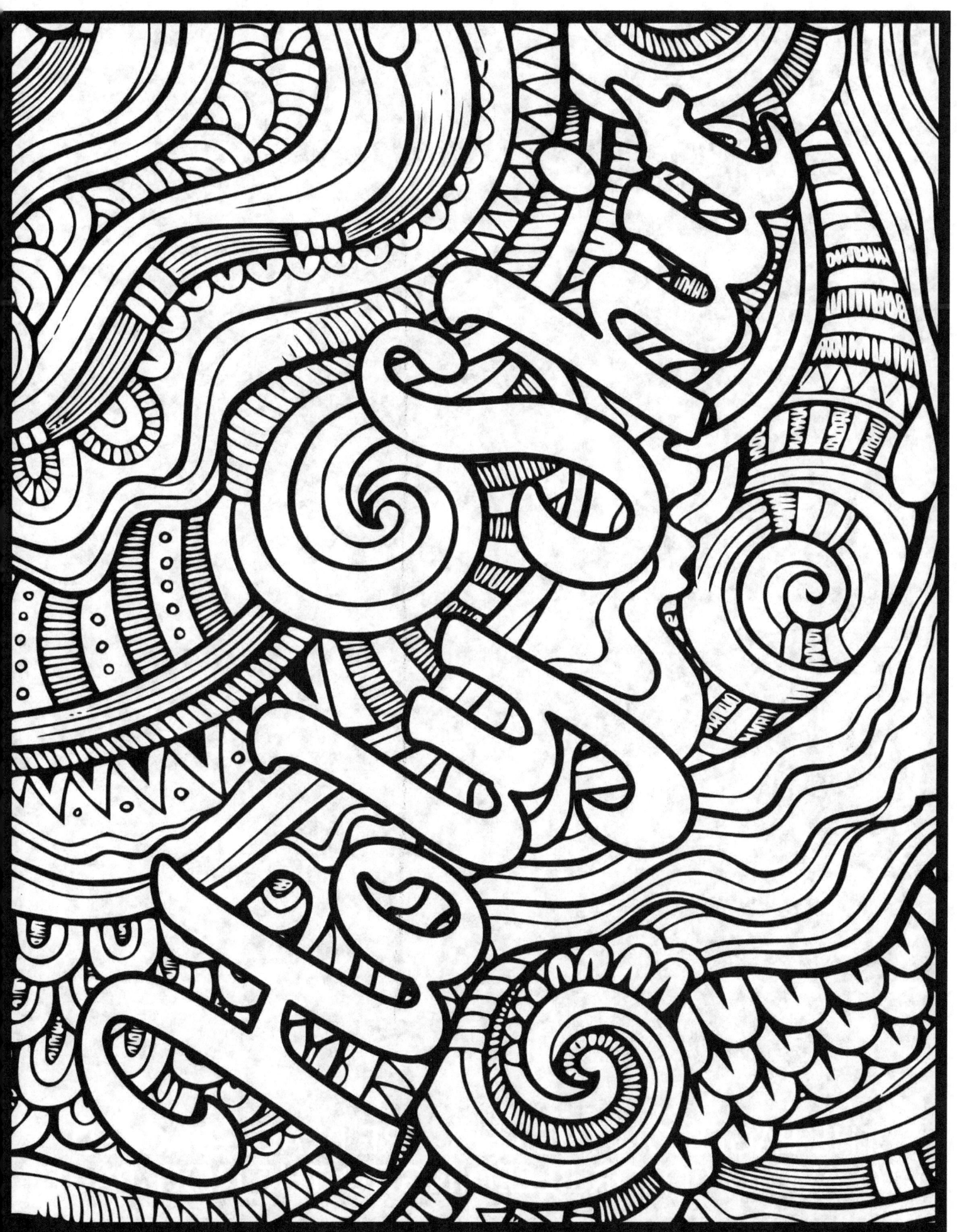

THE PAGES ON THE LEFT ARE BLACK-BACKED TO AVOID COLOR BLEEDING TO THE NEXT PAGE.

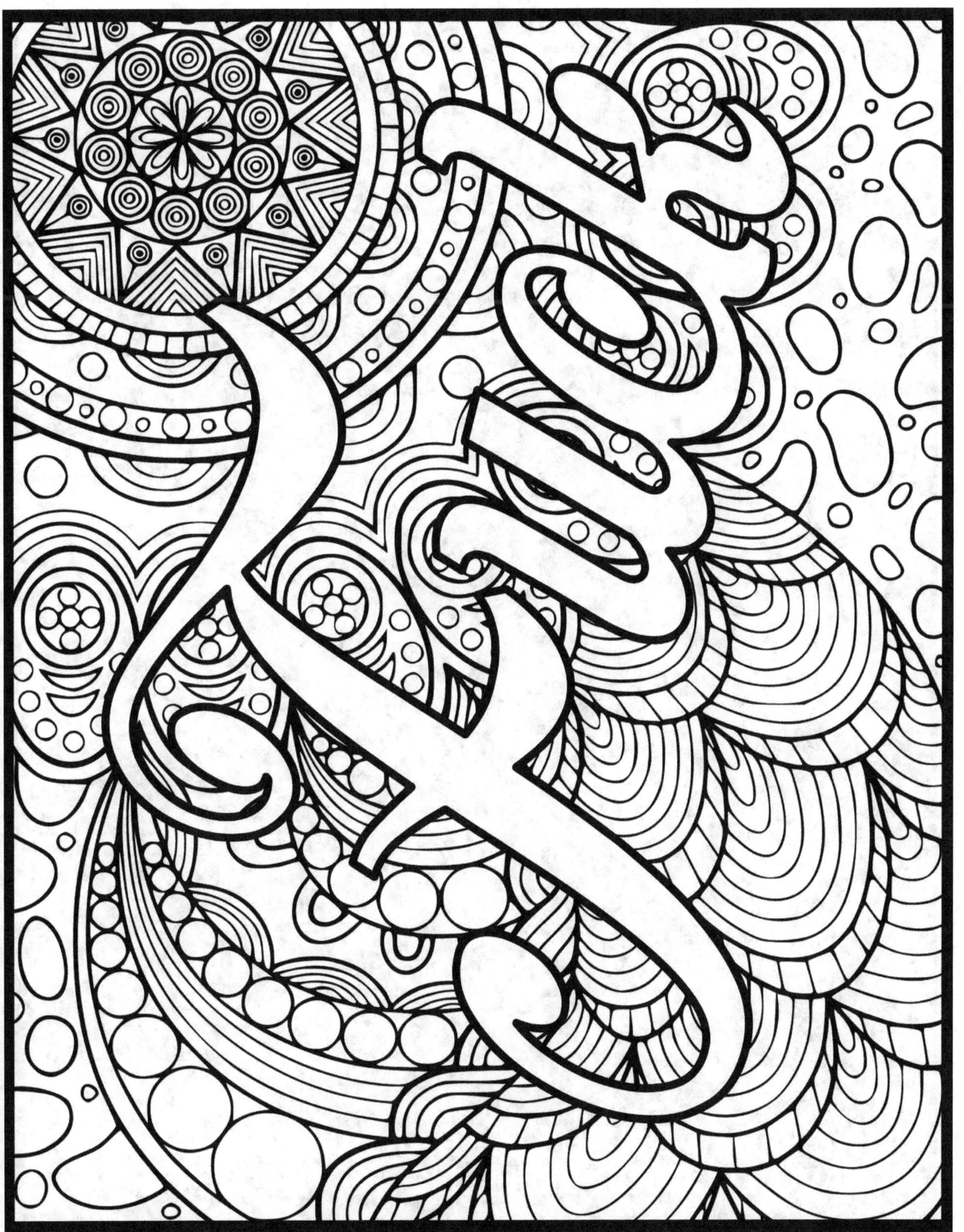

THE PAGES ON THE LEFT ARE BLACK-BACKED
TO AVOID COLOR BLEEDING TO THE NEXT PAGE.

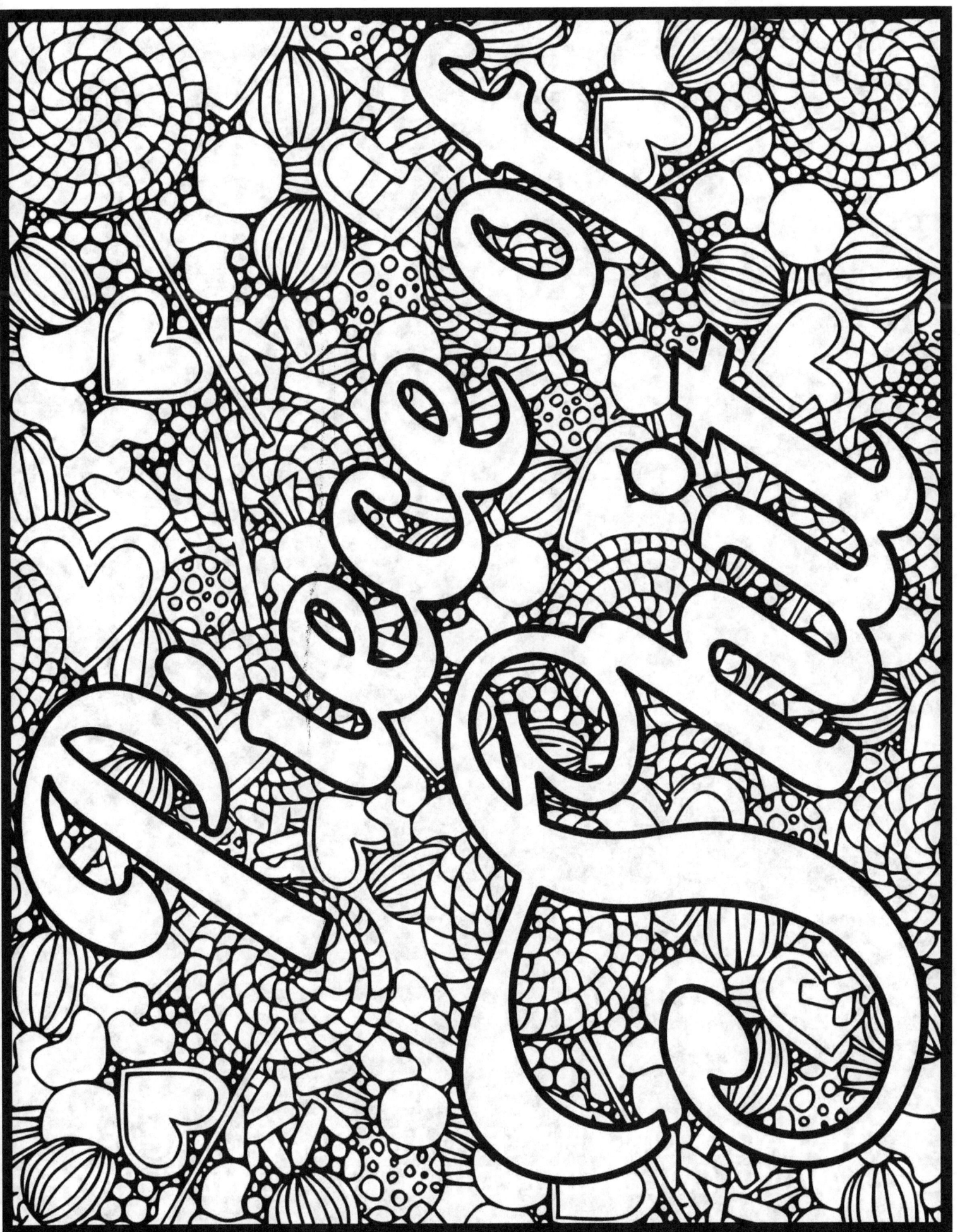

THE PAGES ON THE LEFT ARE BLACK-BACKED
TO AVOID COLOR BLEEDING TO THE NEXT PAGE.

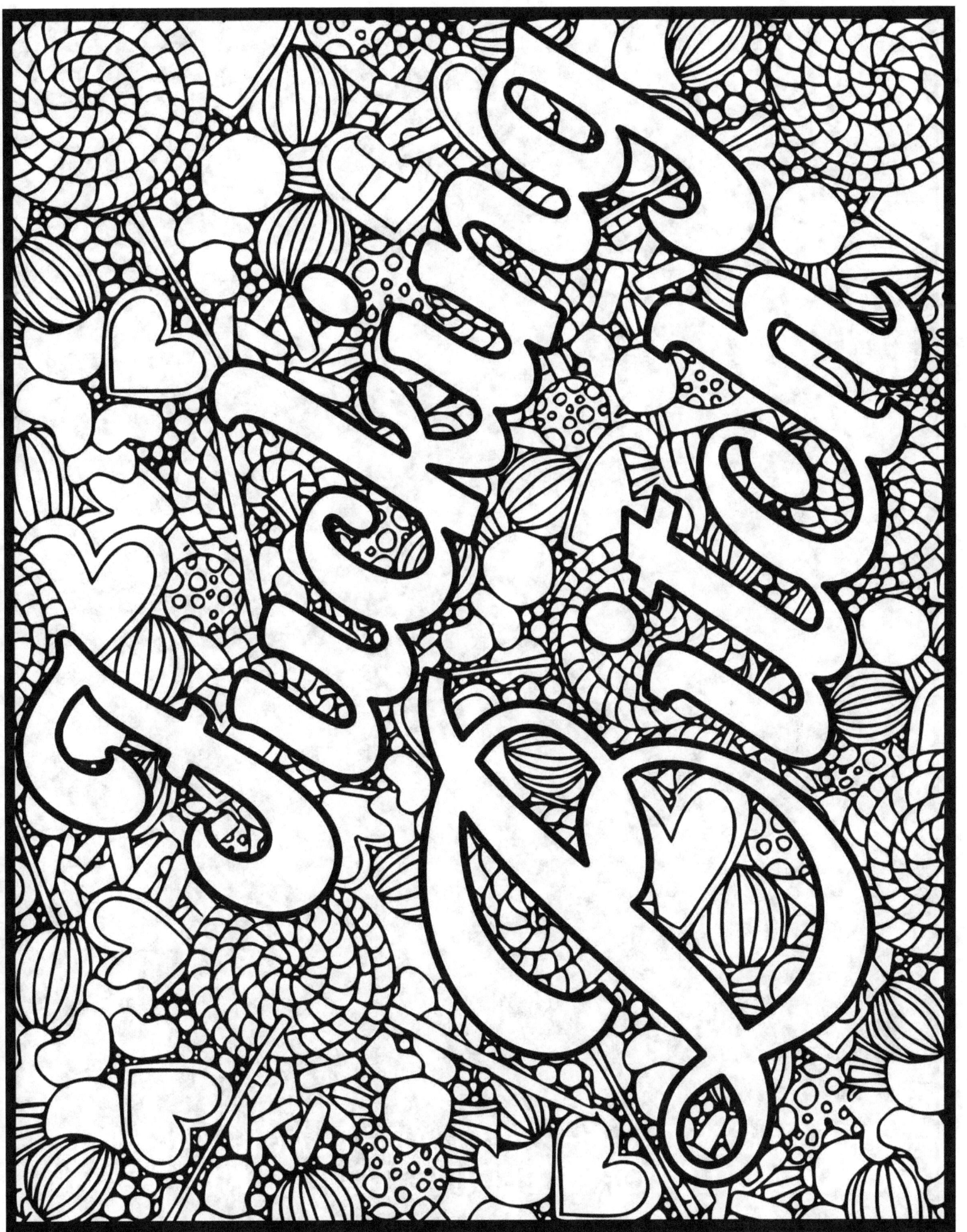

THE PAGES ON THE LEFT ARE BLACK-BACKED TO AVOID COLOR BLEEDING TO THE NEXT PAGE.

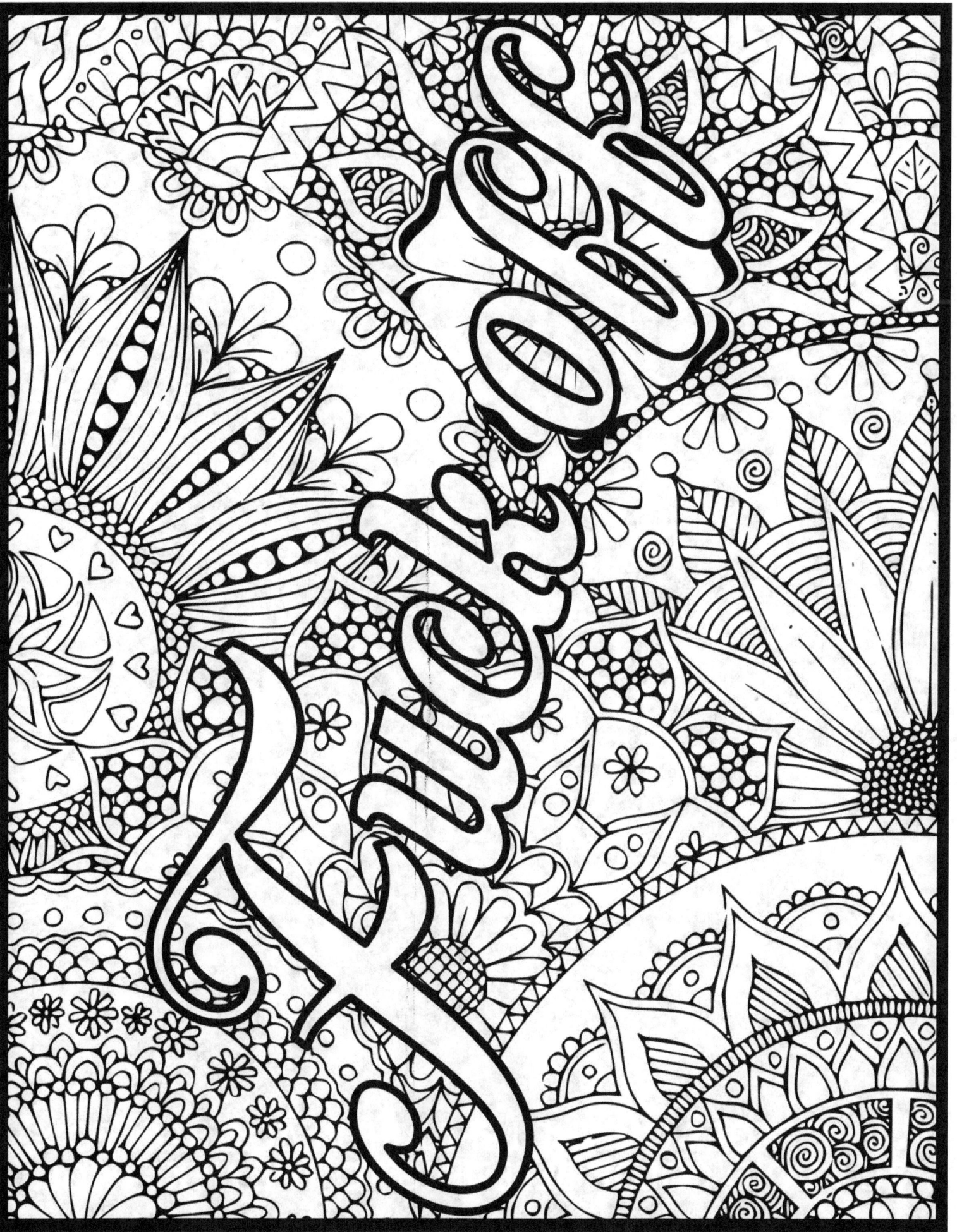

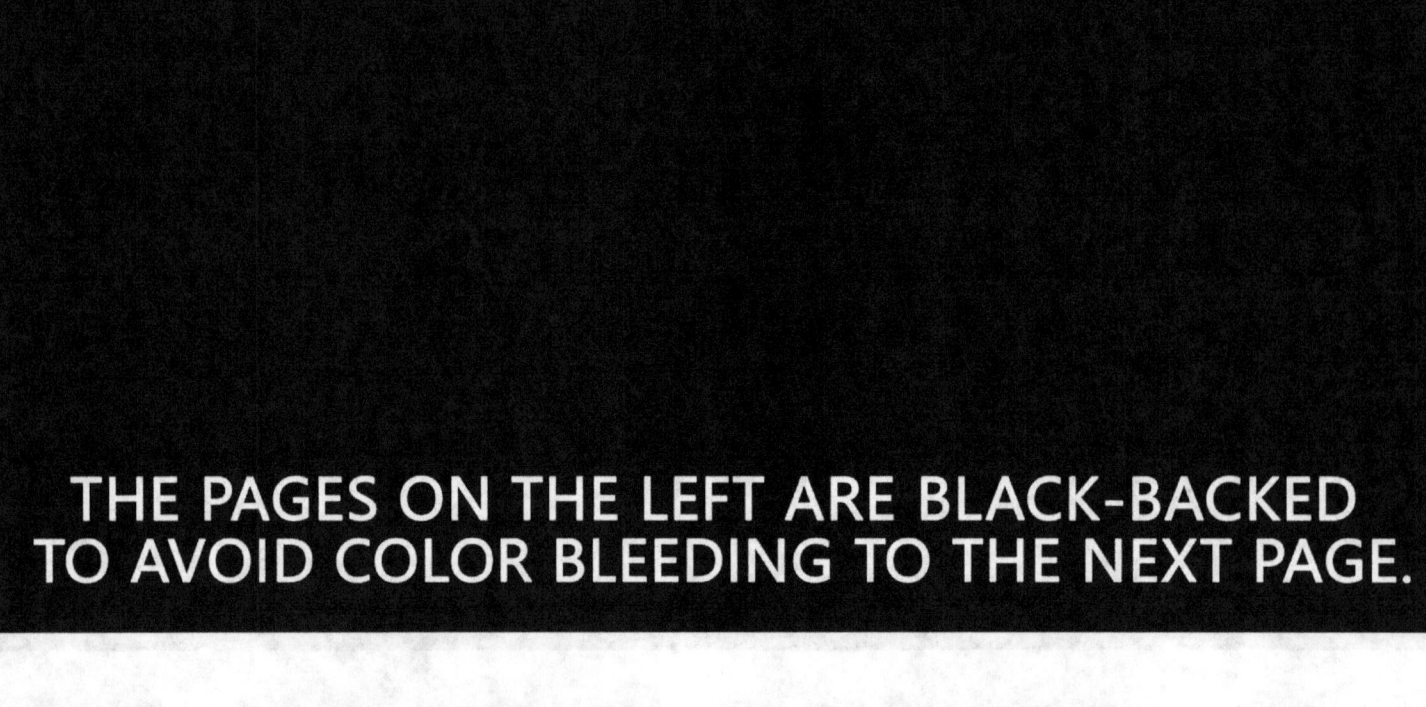

THE PAGES ON THE LEFT ARE BLACK-BACKED
TO AVOID COLOR BLEEDING TO THE NEXT PAGE.

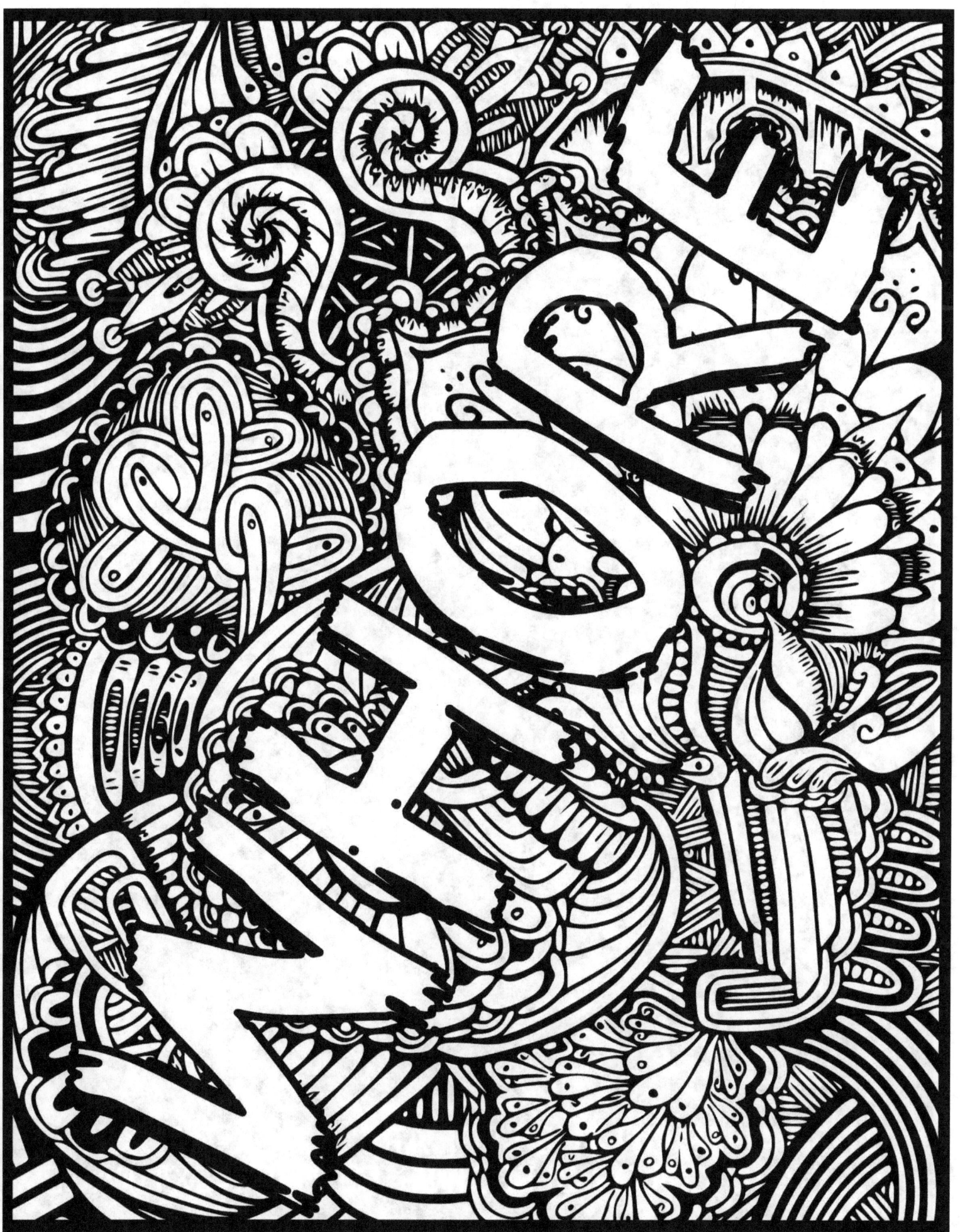

THE PAGES ON THE LEFT ARE BLACK-BACKED
TO AVOID COLOR BLEEDING TO THE NEXT PAGE.

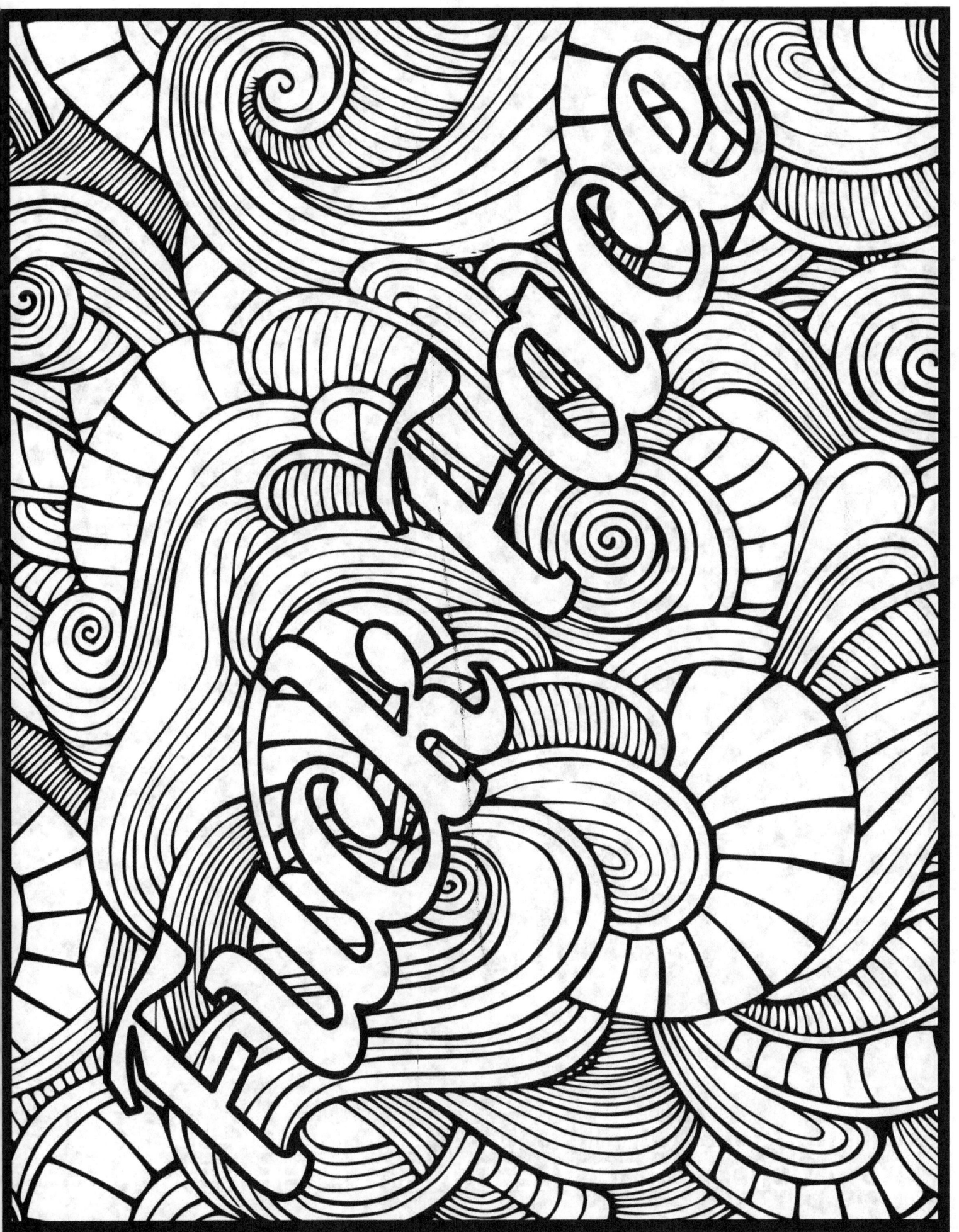

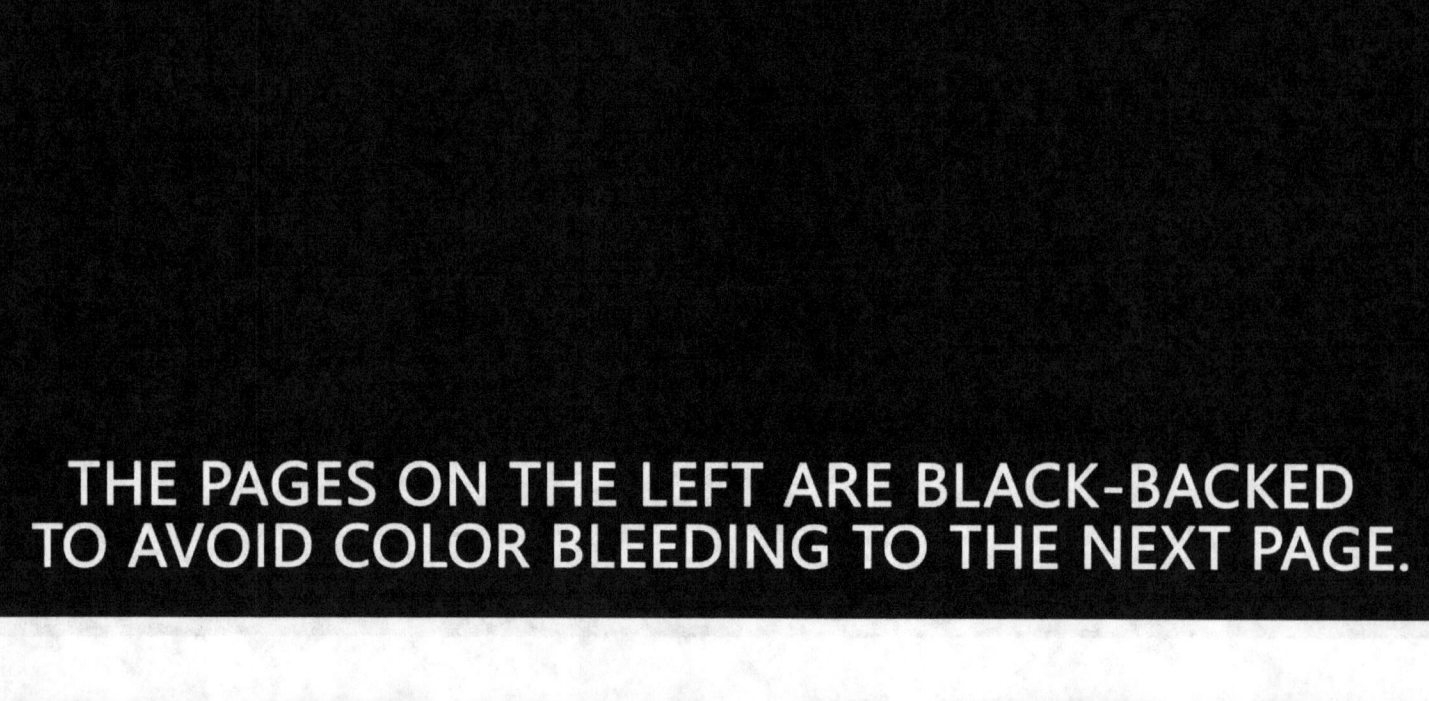

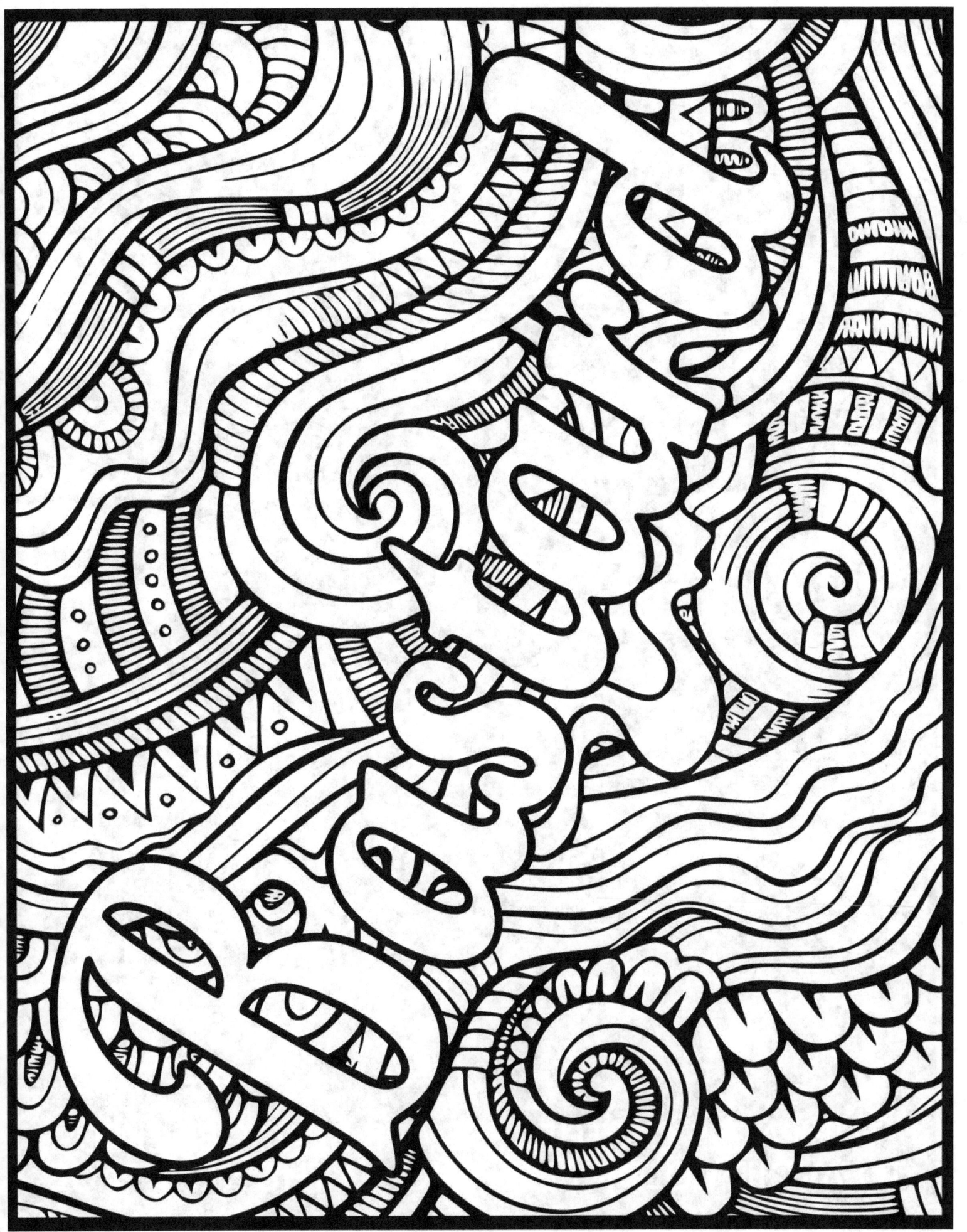

THE PAGES ON THE LEFT ARE BLACK-BACKED
TO AVOID COLOR BLEEDING TO THE NEXT PAGE.

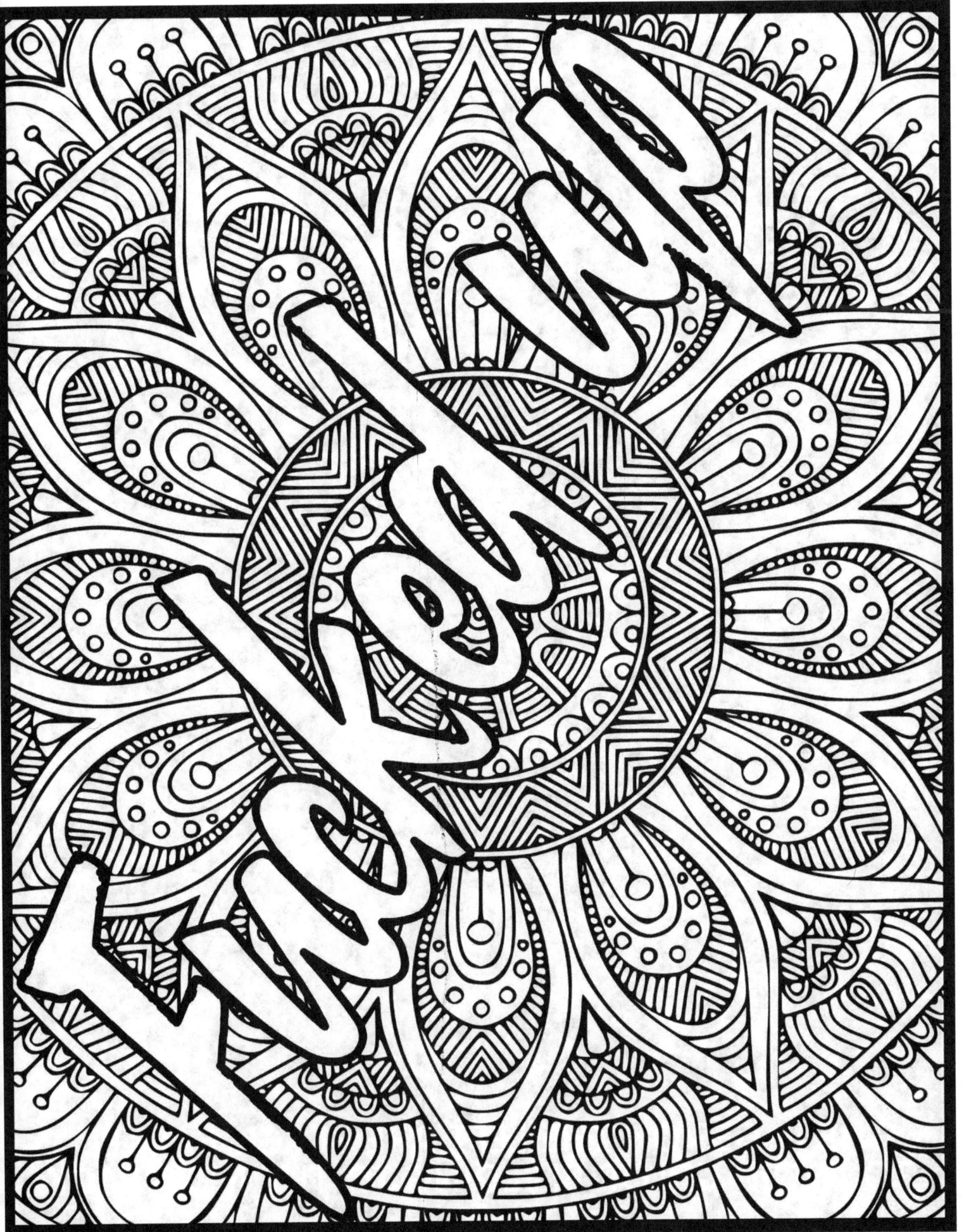

THE PAGES ON THE LEFT ARE BLACK-BACKED
TO AVOID COLOR BLEEDING TO THE NEXT PAGE.

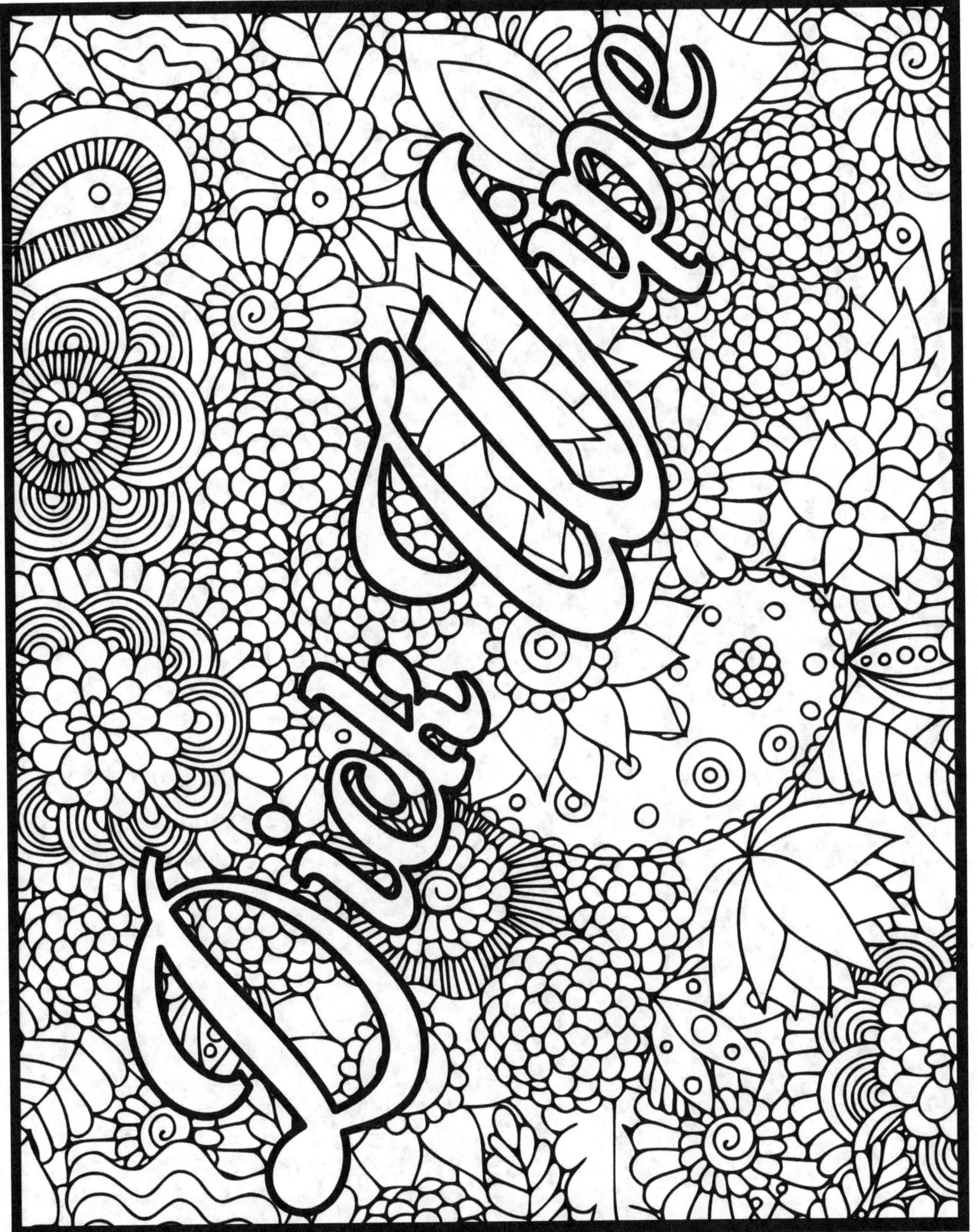

THE PAGES ON THE LEFT ARE BLACK-BACKED TO AVOID COLOR BLEEDING TO THE NEXT PAGE.

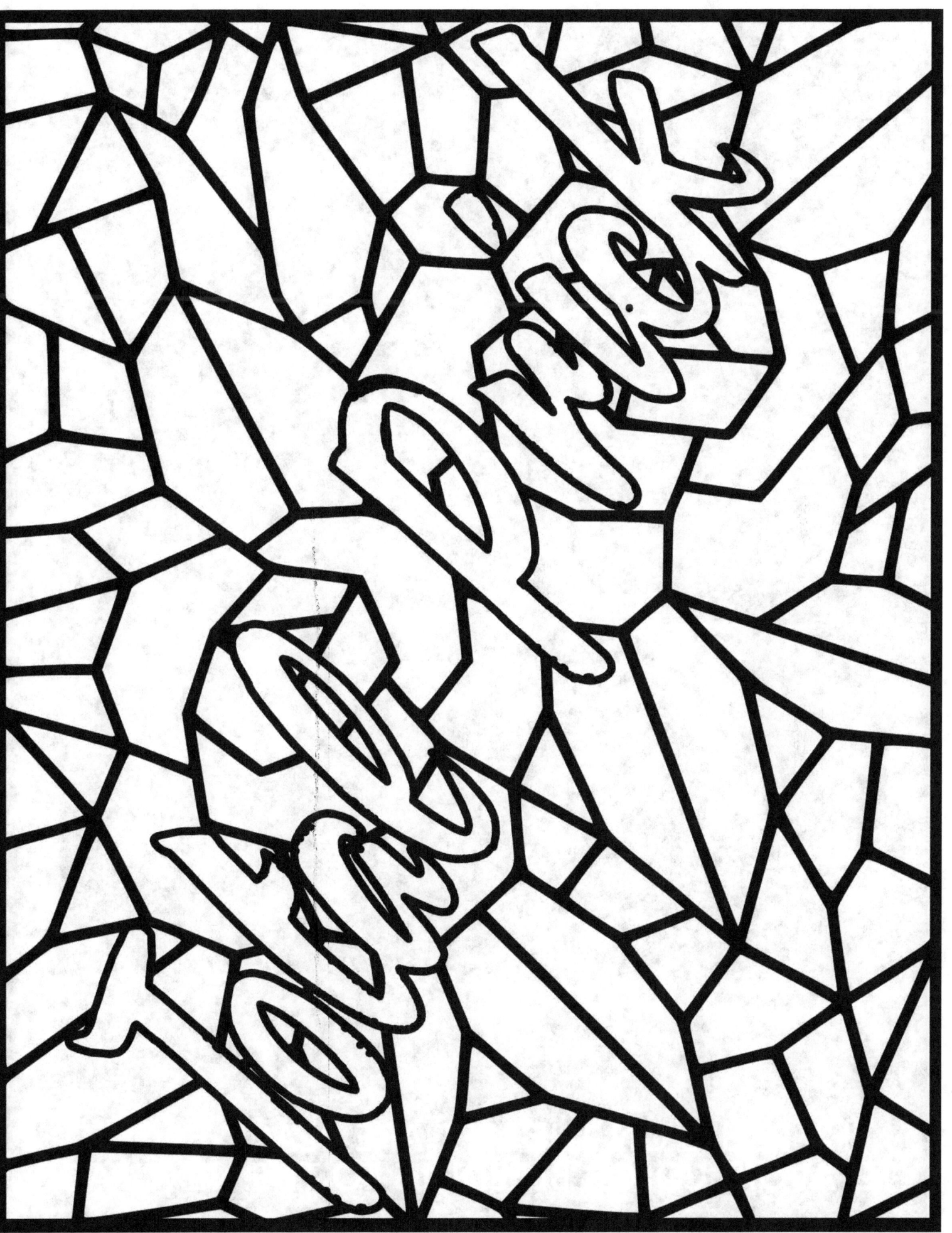

THE PAGES ON THE LEFT ARE BLACK-BACKED
TO AVOID COLOR BLEEDING TO THE NEXT PAGE.

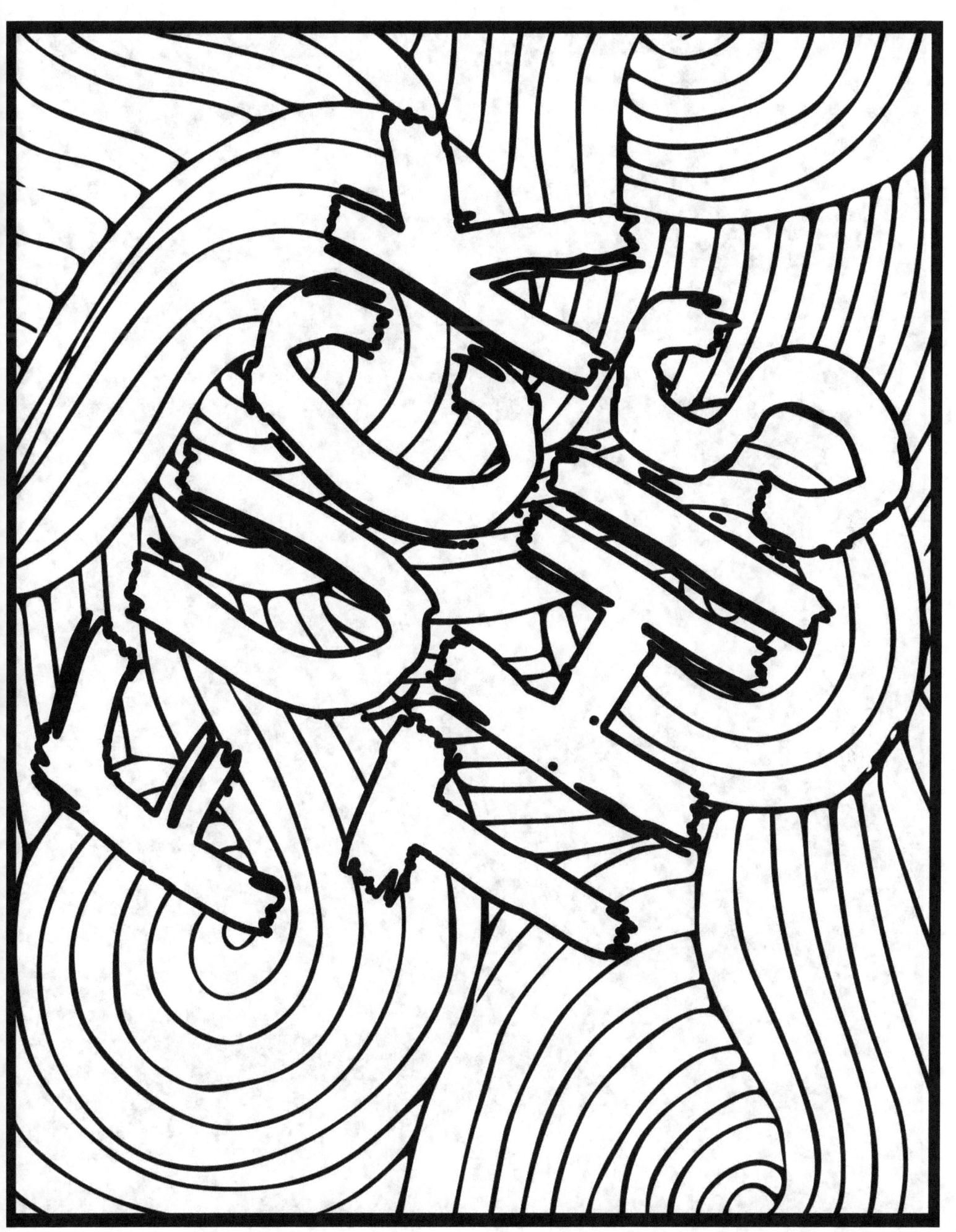

THE PAGES ON THE LEFT ARE BLACK-BACKED
TO AVOID COLOR BLEEDING TO THE NEXT PAGE.

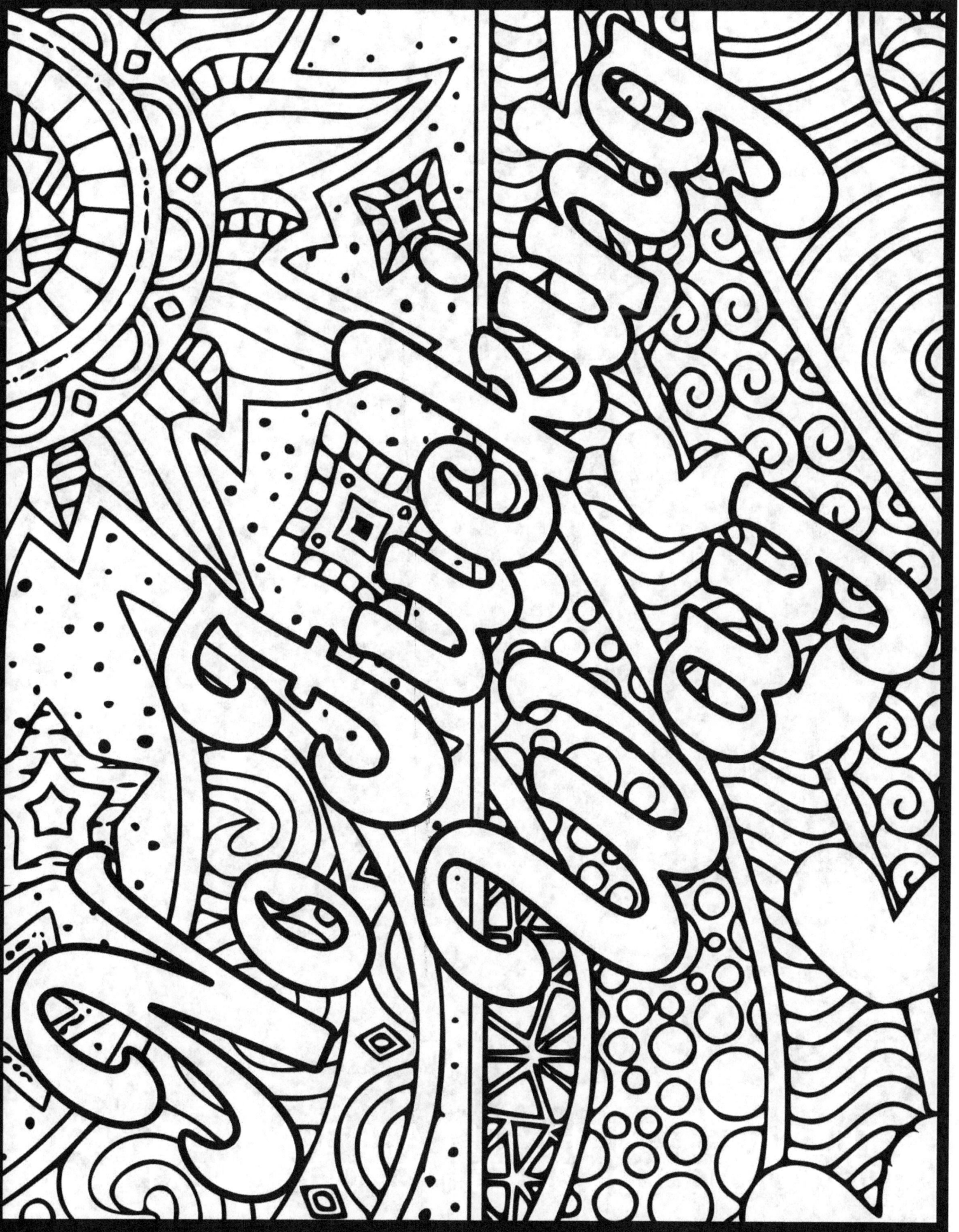

THE PAGES ON THE LEFT ARE BLACK-BACKED
TO AVOID COLOR BLEEDING TO THE NEXT PAGE.

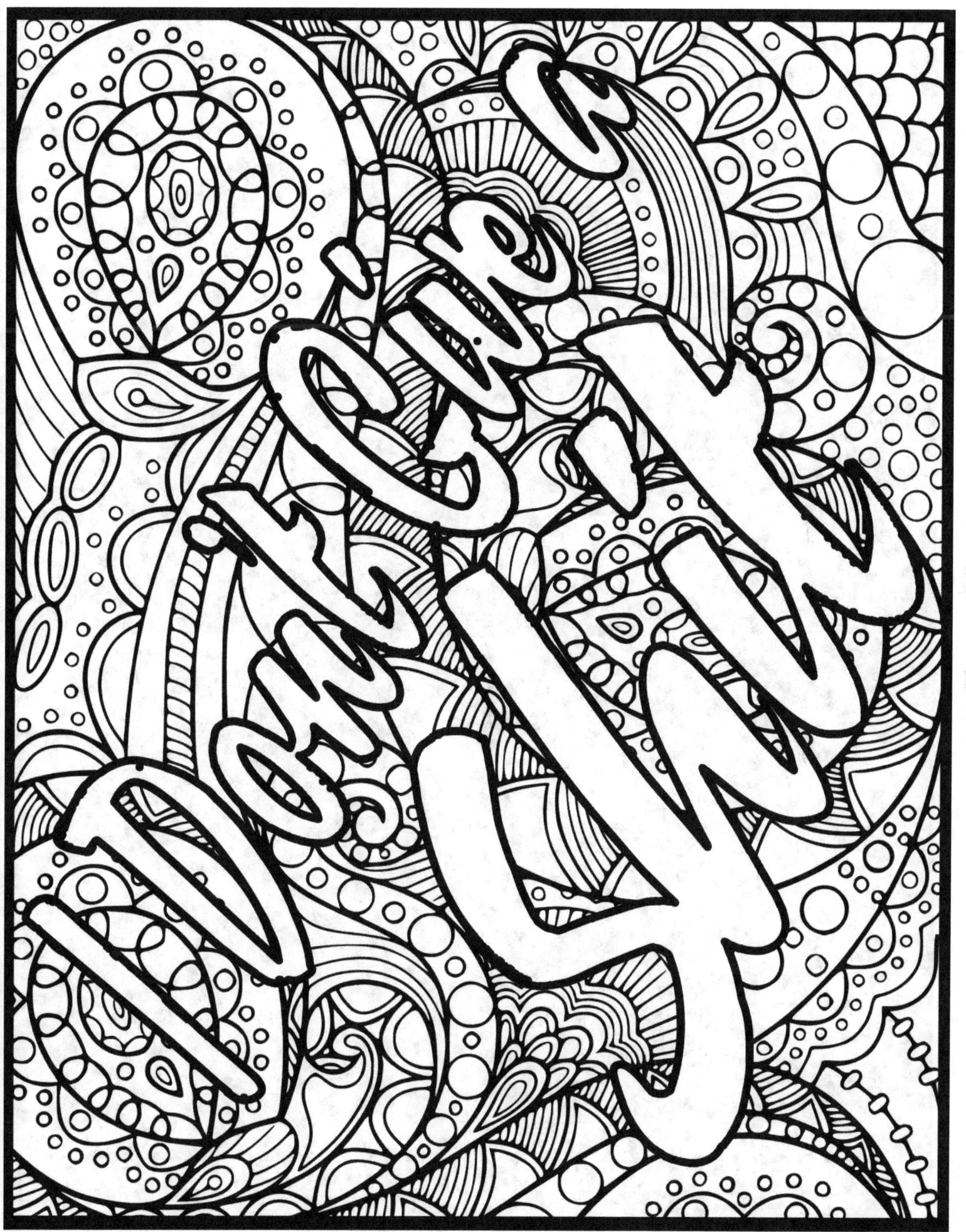

THE PAGES ON THE LEFT ARE BLACK-BACKED TO AVOID COLOR BLEEDING TO THE NEXT PAGE.

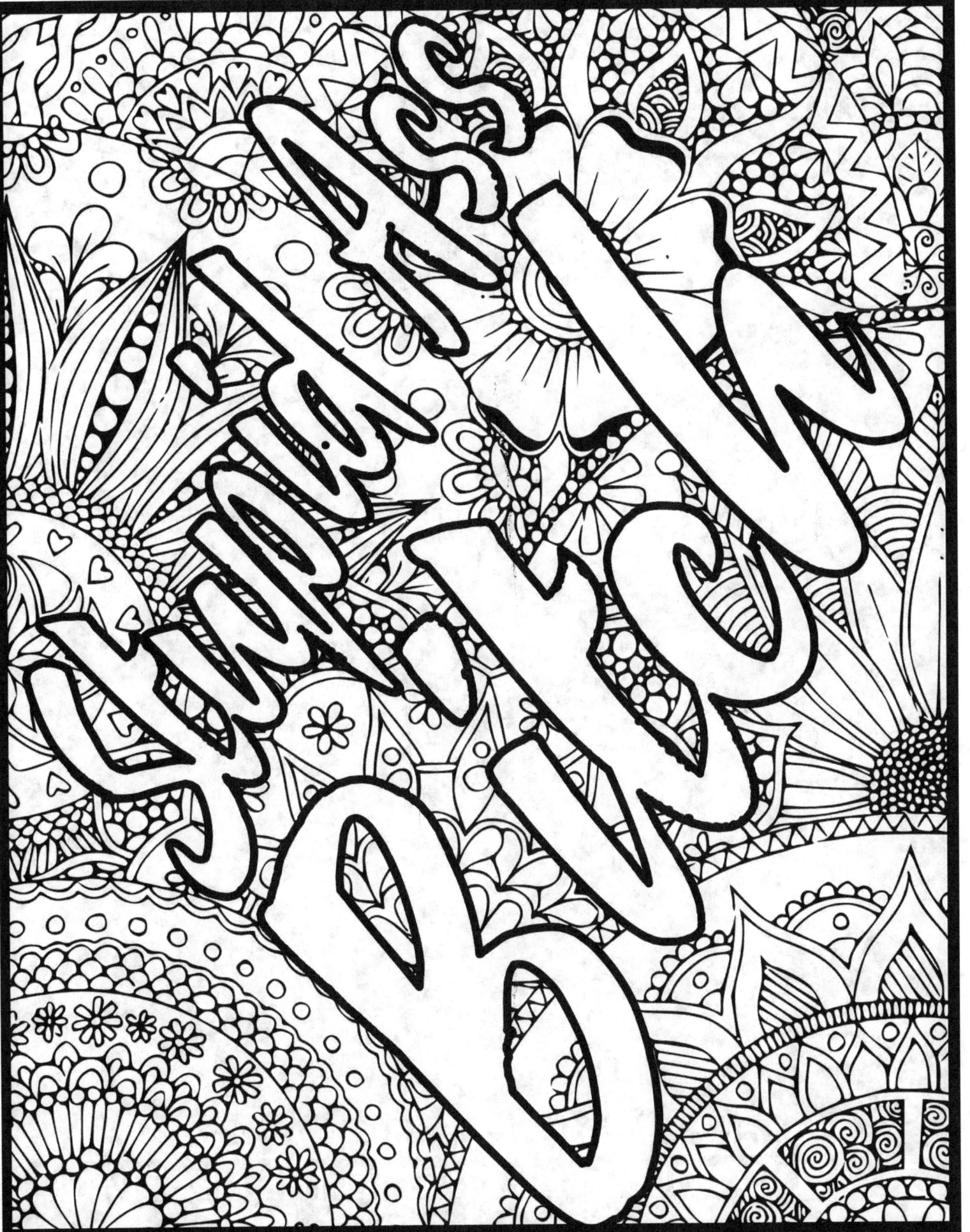

THE PAGES ON THE LEFT ARE BLACK-BACKED
TO AVOID COLOR BLEEDING TO THE NEXT PAGE.

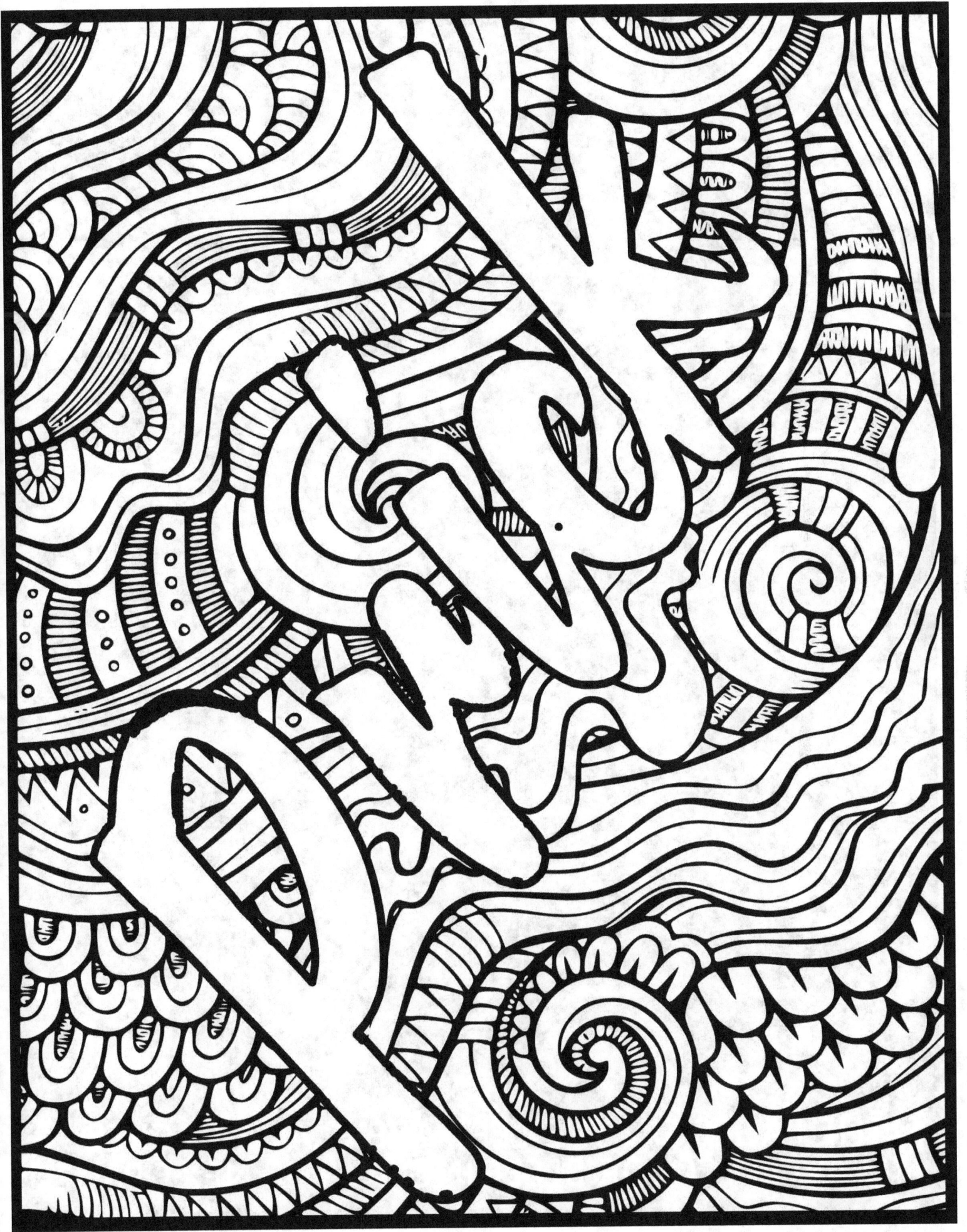

THE PAGES ON THE LEFT ARE BLACK-BACKED
TO AVOID COLOR BLEEDING TO THE NEXT PAGE.

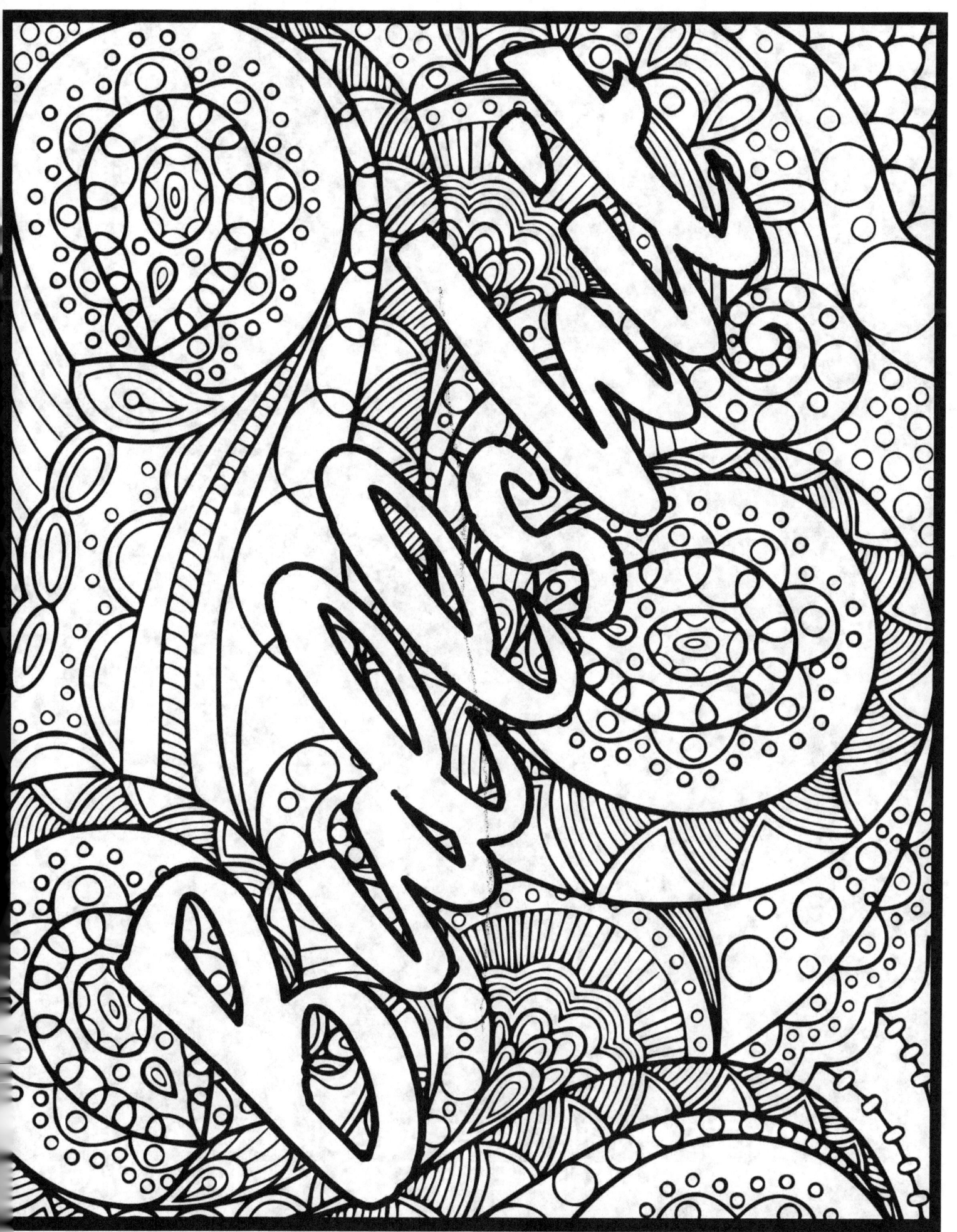

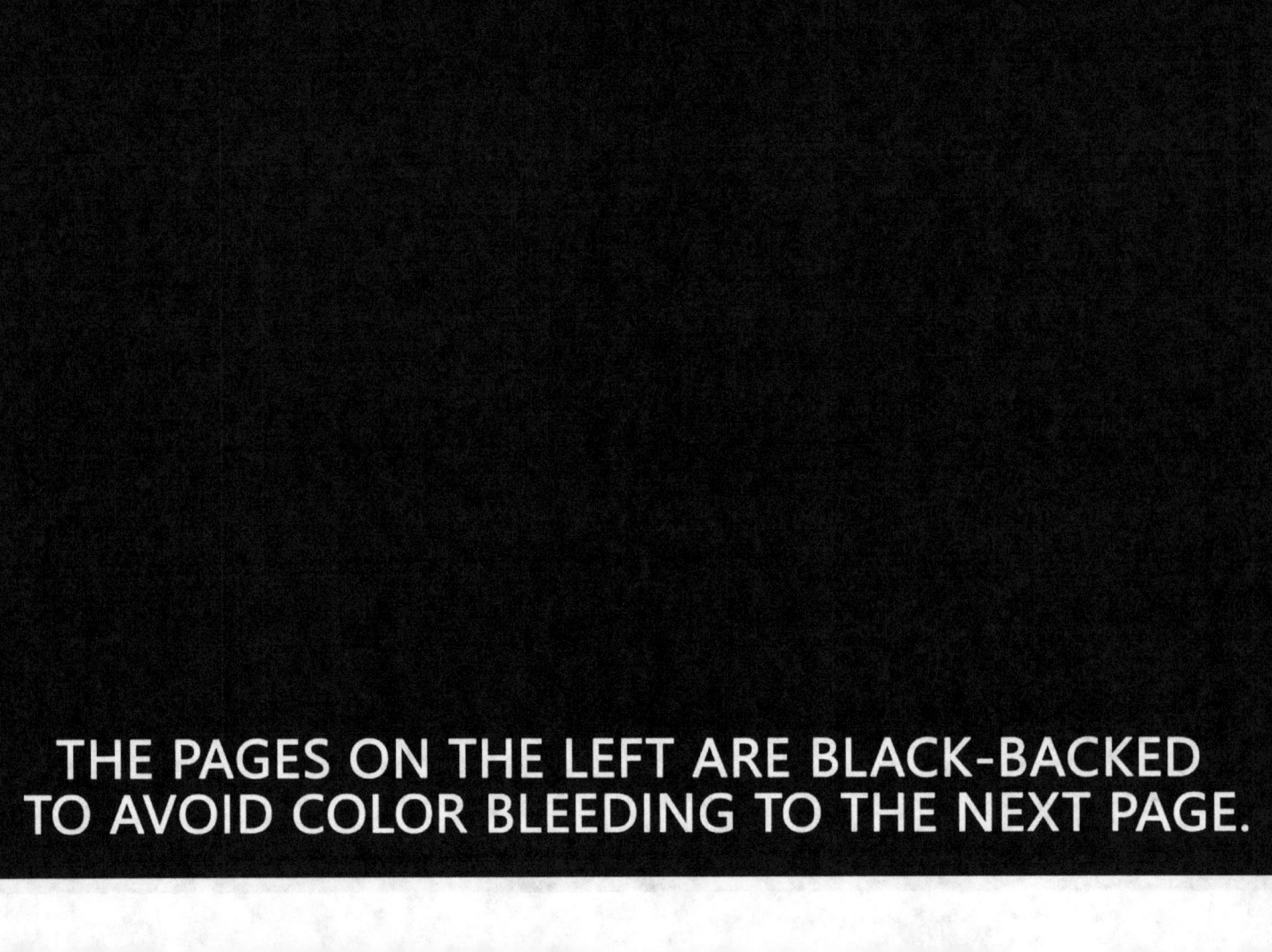

THE PAGES ON THE LEFT ARE BLACK-BACKED
TO AVOID COLOR BLEEDING TO THE NEXT PAGE.

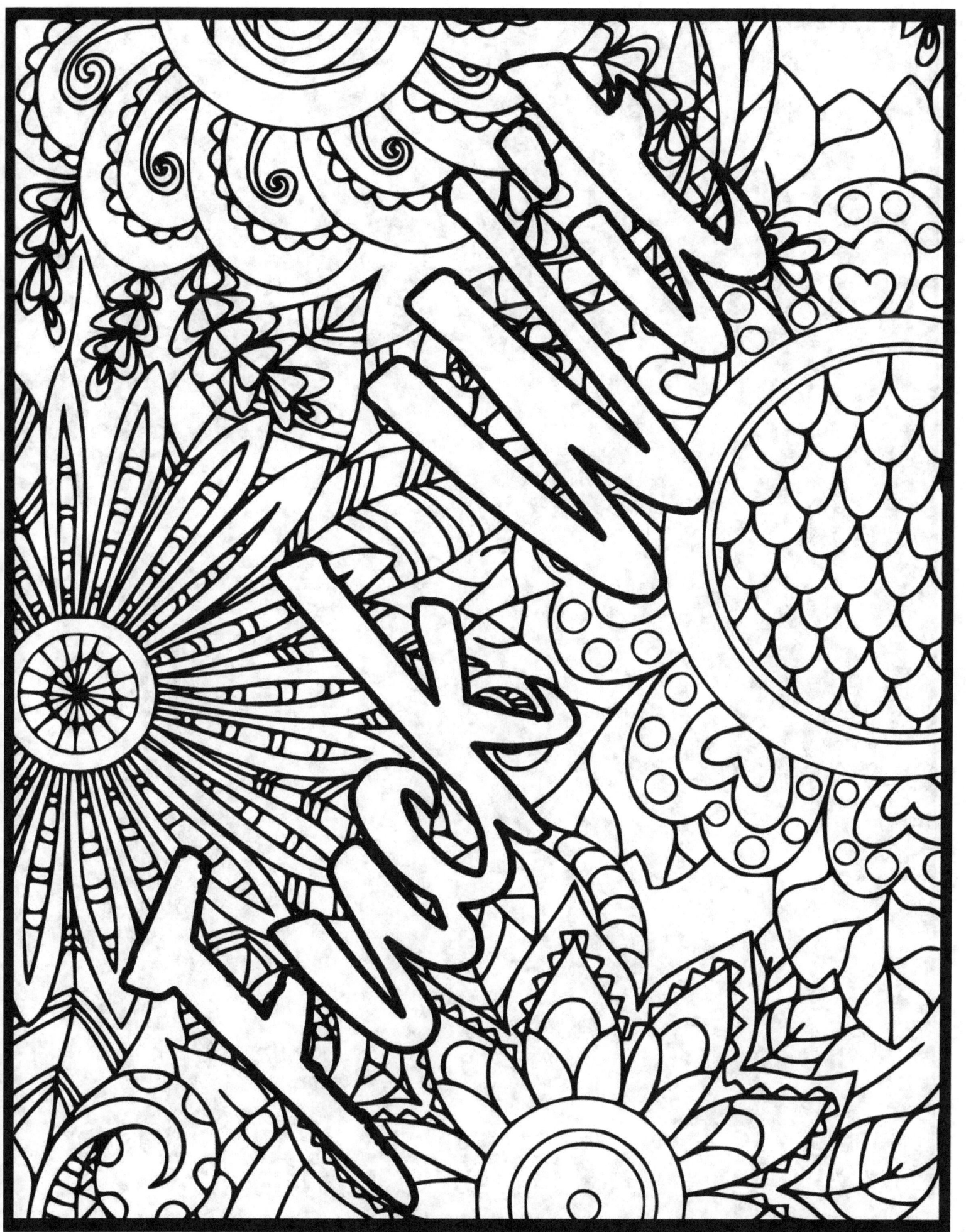

THE PAGES ON THE LEFT ARE BLACK-BACKED
TO AVOID COLOR BLEEDING TO THE NEXT PAGE.

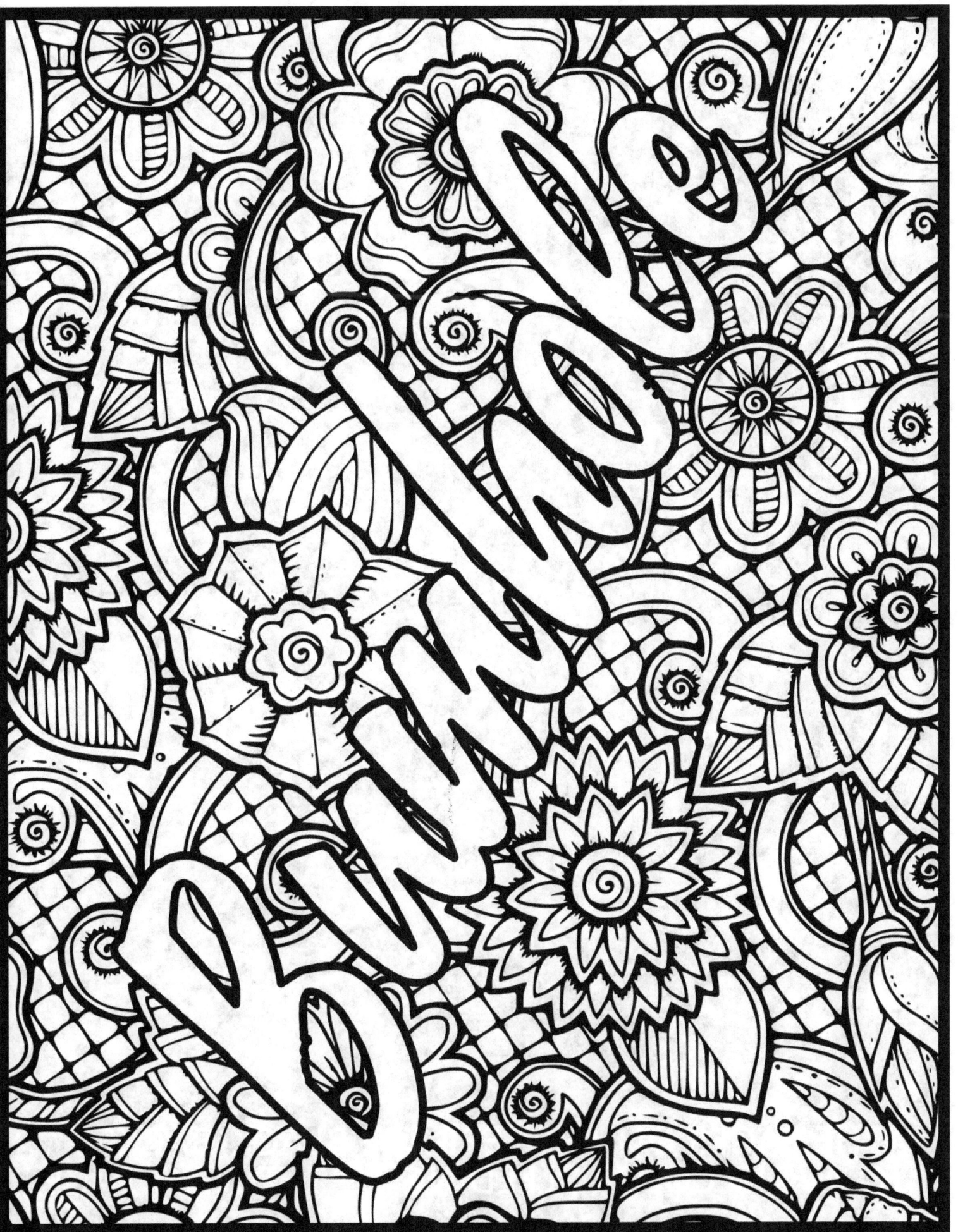

THE PAGES ON THE LEFT ARE BLACK-BACKED
TO AVOID COLOR BLEEDING TO THE NEXT PAGE.

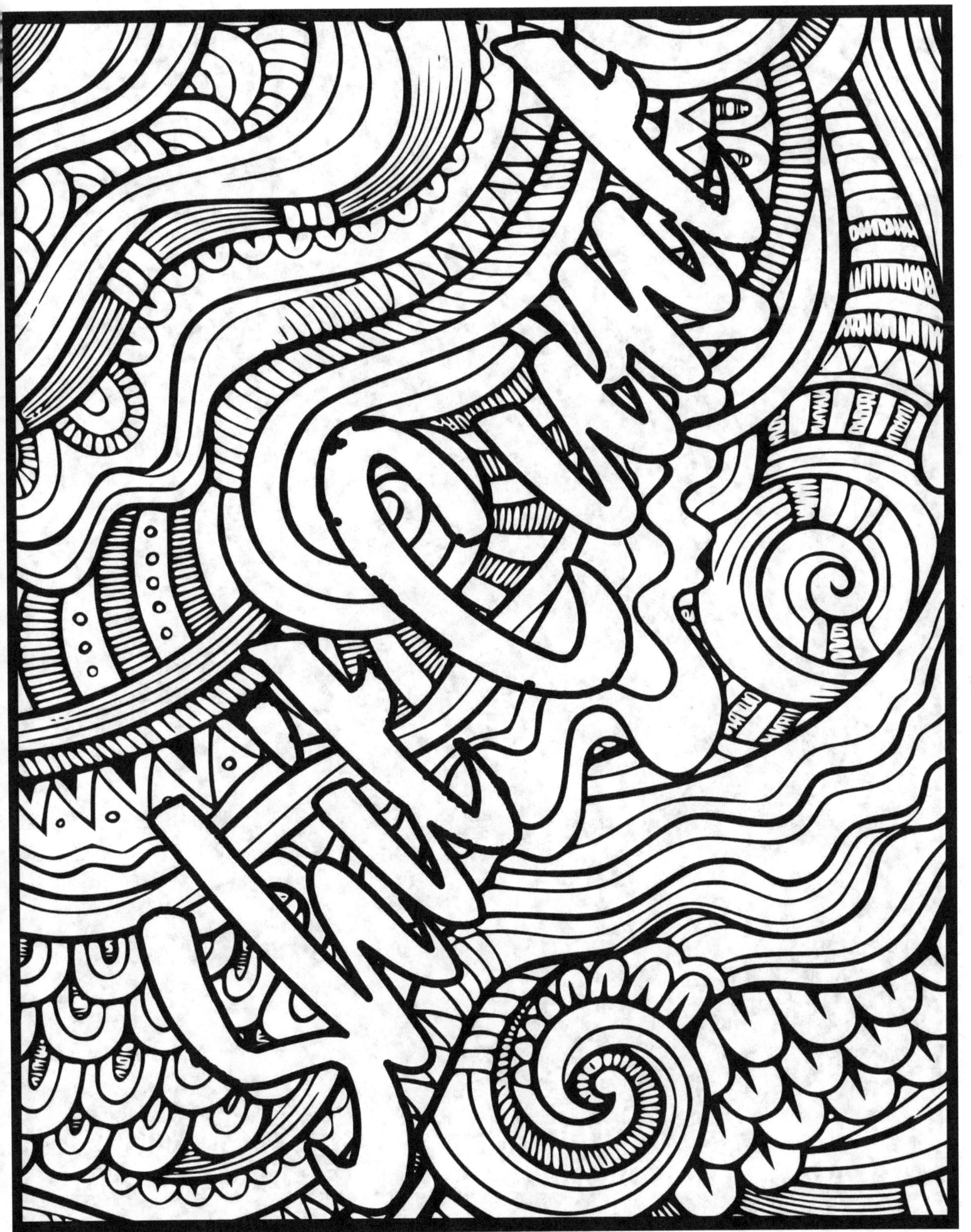

THE PAGES ON THE LEFT ARE BLACK-BACKED
TO AVOID COLOR BLEEDING TO THE NEXT PAGE.

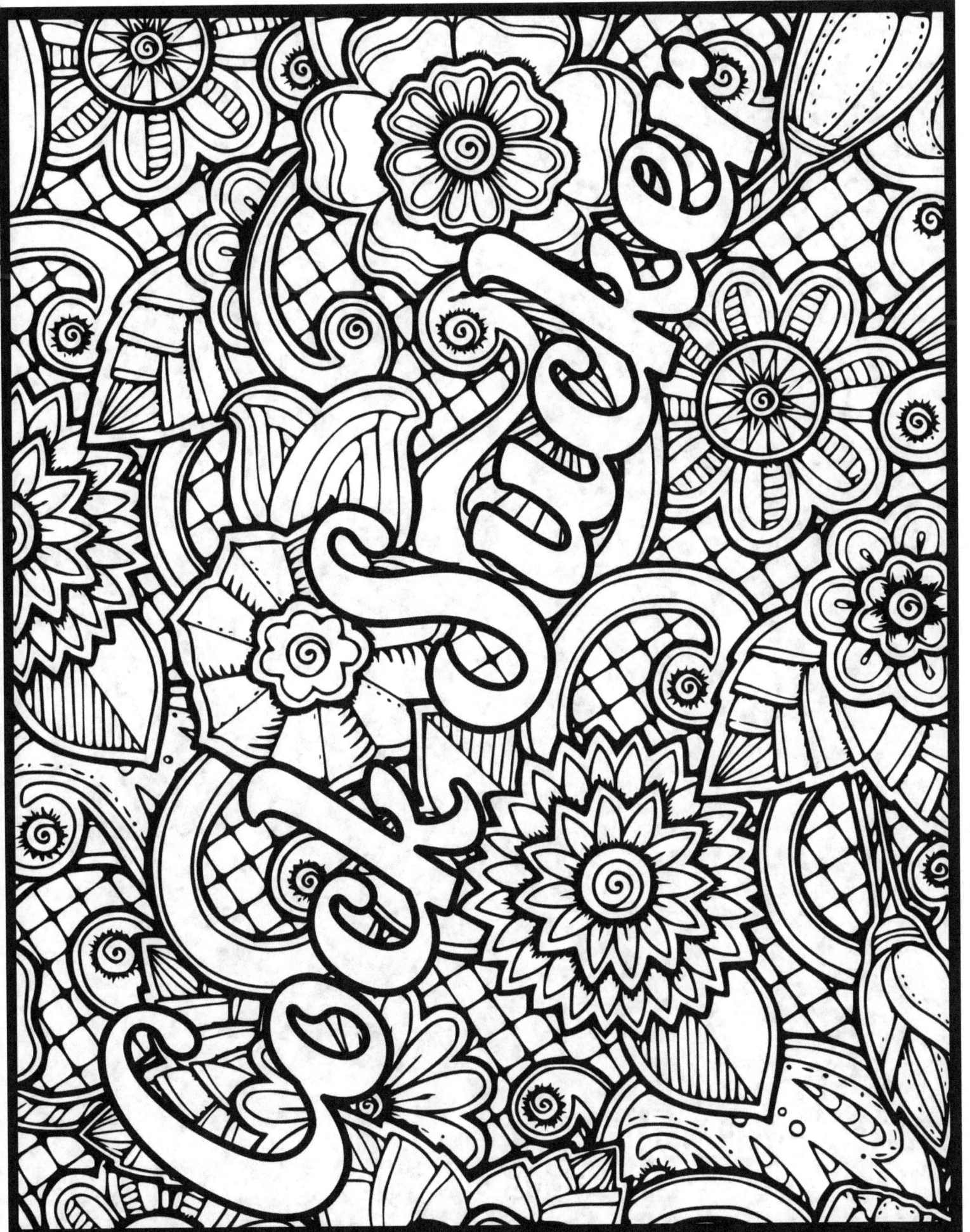

THE PAGES ON THE LEFT ARE BLACK-BACKED TO AVOID COLOR BLEEDING TO THE NEXT PAGE.

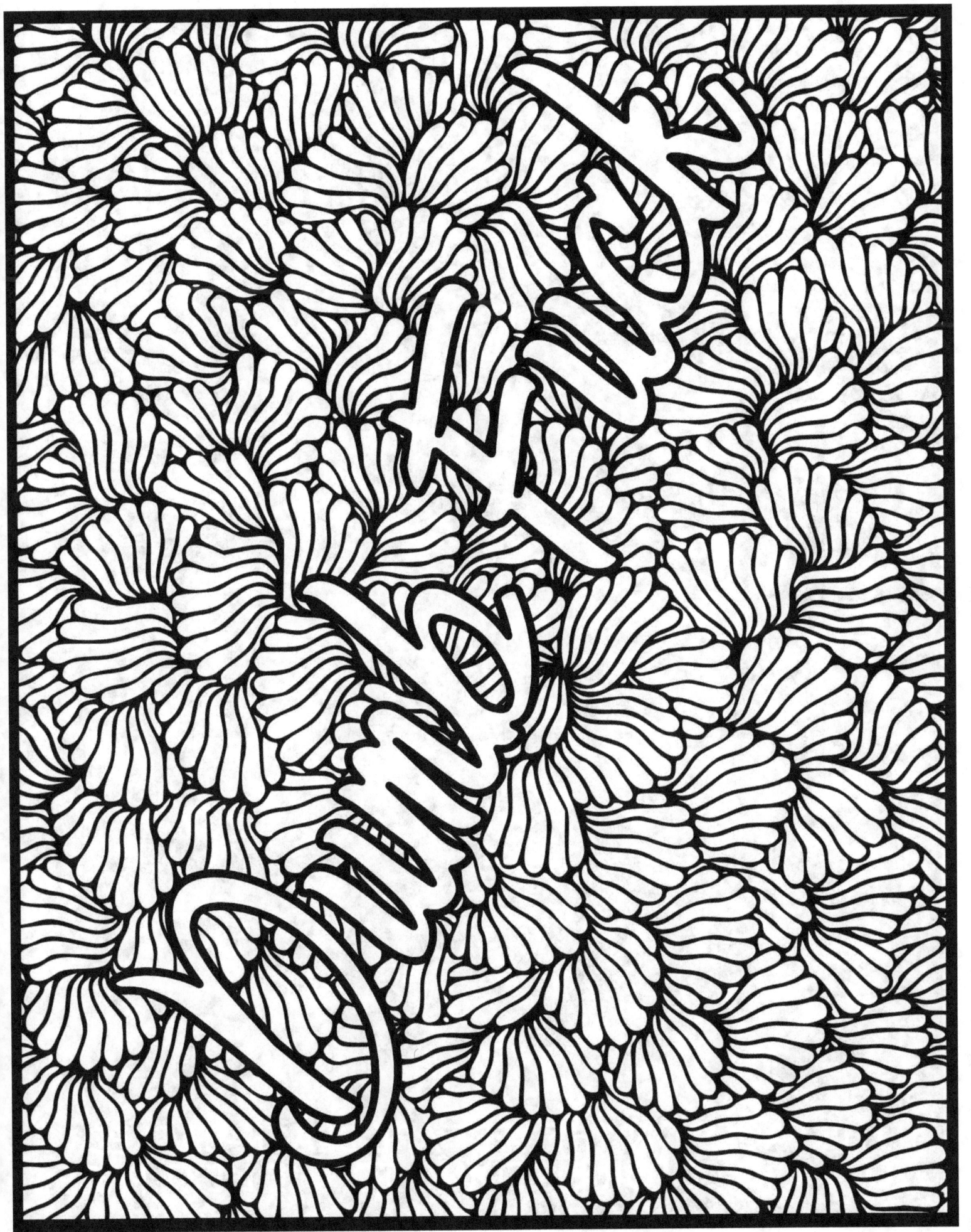

THE PAGES ON THE LEFT ARE BLACK-BACKED TO AVOID COLOR BLEEDING TO THE NEXT PAGE.

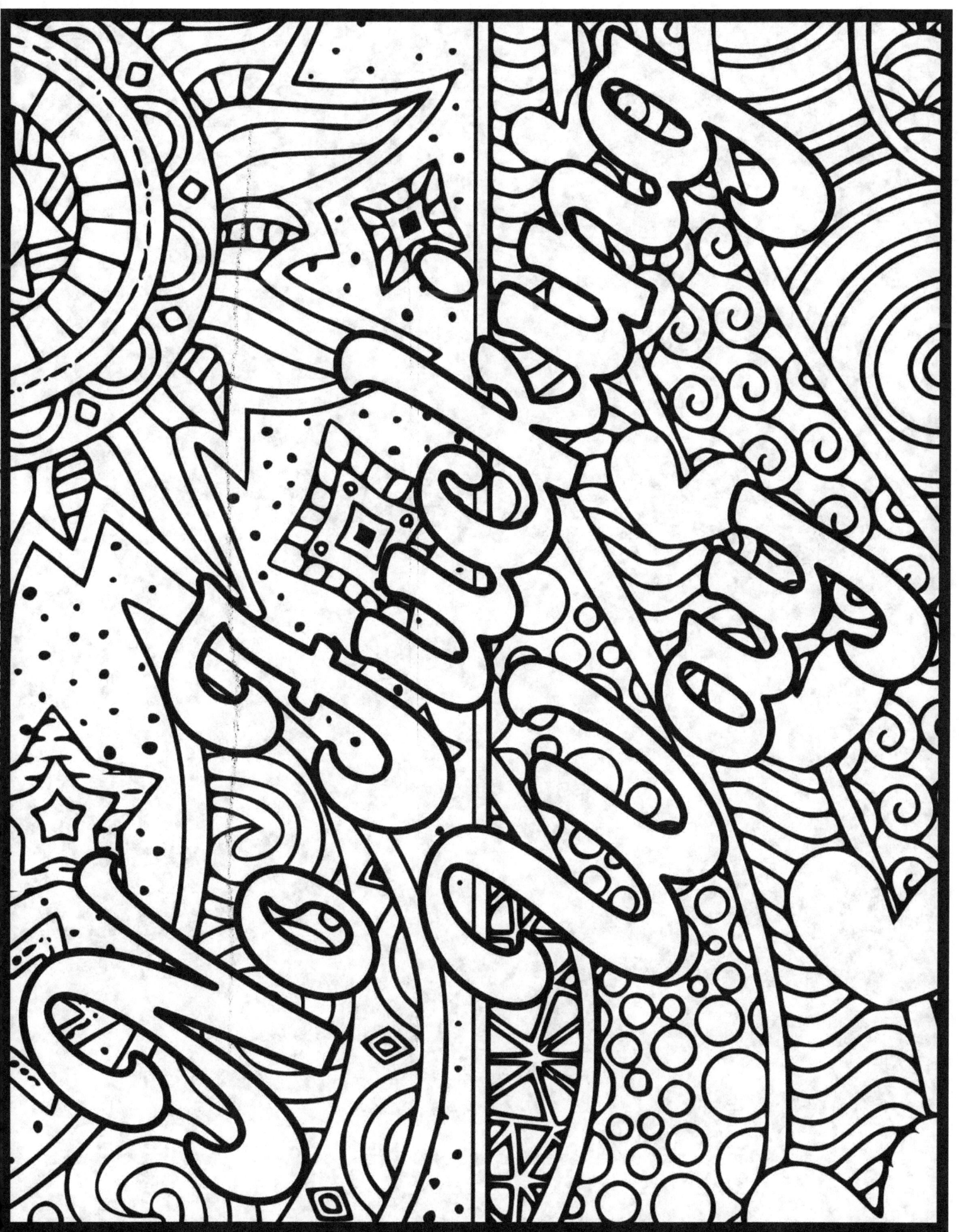

**THE PAGES ON THE LEFT ARE BLACK-BACKED
TO AVOID COLOR BLEEDING TO THE NEXT PAGE.**

www.ingramcontent.com/pod-product-compliance
Lightning Source LLC
Chambersburg PA
CBHW060435220526
45465CB00008B/3143